BEHIND
the STORIES

BETHANYHOUSE

Published by Bethany House Publishers
A Ministry of Bethany Fellowship International
11400 Hampshire Avenue South
Bloomington, Minnesota 55438
www.bethanyhouse.com

Printed in the United States of America by
Bethany Press International, Bloomington, Minnesota 55438

Library of Congress Cataloging-in-Publication Data

Eble, Diane.
     Behind the stories: Christian novelists reveal the heart in the art of their writing / by Diane Eble.
          p.   cm.
     ISBN 0-7642-2463-8 (pbk.)
     1. Christian fiction—Authorship. I. Title.
     PN3377.5.C47 E24   2002
     808.3—dc21   2001005584

To all novelists—
past, present, and future—
who are Christians,
whether their names appear in this book or not.

"Stories are medicine," said Clarissa Pinkola Estes.
May your stories always bring healing to a broken world
and glory to Jesus Christ.

Contents

Introduction. 9

1. Say Yes to God
   Bill Myers: Just Say Yes   12
   Sharon Foster: The Other Side of Fear   20
   Randy Alcorn: A Matter of Perspective.   28
2. Uniquely Gifted
   Jim Walker: Obedient to God's Design   36
   Robin Jones Gunn: Reaching "Teens in the Tent"   42
3. Everybody Needs Somebody
   Judith Pella: With a Little Help From a Friend   50
   Melody Carlson: Honor the Gift   56
   Jamie Langston Turner: Influenced and Influencing   62
4. Dream God's Dreams
   Karen Kingsbury: Reach for the Stars.   70
   Catherine Palmer: Fairy Tales and Faith   76
   Jane Peart: Delight Yourself in the Lord   82
   Alton Gansky: Despite the Obstacles.   88
   Lawana Blackwell: Never Too Late   94
5. Not By My Strength
   Janette Oke: Keys to Ministry 100
   Linda Chaikin: Yielding. 106
   Lori Copeland: A Willing Heart. 112
6. Redeeming the Past
   Patricia Hickman: Flying Lessons 118
   Lynn Marzulli: Redeeming the Darkness. 128
   Robin Lee Hatcher: No Compromise. 132
   Angela Elwell Hunt: Nothing Wasted in God's Economy. . . 140

7. Obedient to One Voice
   Patricia Sprinkle: Embracing the Joy 148
   Bodie Thoene: Despite Disability 154
   Terri Blackstock: Waking Up 160
   Athol Dickson: The Test 172
8. God's Stretching Places
   Francine Rivers: What God Took Away 182
   Jan Karon: Through the Fire 188
   Jane Kirkpatrick: Into the Wilderness and Beyond 194
   Anne de Graaf: The More Difficult Road 204
   Lisa Tawn Bergren: Out of the Comfort Zone 210
   Beverly Lewis: Choices.................................. 216
   Peggy Stoks: Juggling an "Embarrassment of Riches" 224
9. Perseverance and Hard Work
   Dee Henderson: The Plans of the Diligent............... 232
   Gilbert Morris: Step by Step in Faith 238
   Jack Cavanaugh: The Long Wait 242
10. Success: True and False
    T. Davis Bunn: Two Kinds of Success 250
    Liz Curtis Higgs: Signposts of Joy 256
    Jerry B. Jenkins: The Test of Success 262
11. God's Gracious Ways
    Diane Noble: Led in the Path of Mercy.................. 270
    Penelope J. Stokes: Connecting with God 276
    Deborah Raney: The Gracious Hand of the Lord 284

Introduction

Back in 1980 or so, I read an article by Harold Fickett that stirred something deep within me. I don't recall exactly where the article appeared, but I think it was in a trade journal for the Christian publishing industry. Fickett wrote about the power of story and urged Christian publishers to take a chance on publishing fiction. At the time, the only fiction that was being published was a bit of biblical fiction and Janette Oke's prairie romances. Fickett urged Christian publishers to cultivate authors of fiction who were Christian, to provide a place for them to go to develop their craft.

The article impressed me so much that I began to pray right then that God would do just what Harold Fickett had proposed. Now, twenty years later, Christian fiction is booming. Authors are honing their craft, even beginning to make an impact on the culture around them. That was Harold Fickett's dream, and mine, and it looks like slowly but surely it is being realized.

In a modest way, I may have had a small part in the answer to my own prayer. When the opportunity came for me to be the writer for Tyndale House Publisher's *PageTurner's Journal,* I jumped at the chance. Over the past several years, I have had the privilege of getting to know writers such as Francine Rivers, B. J. Hoff, Lori Copeland, Catherine Palmer, Jerry Jenkins, Michael Phillips, Janette Oke, and many others. As they told me their stories, it struck me that each person's situation held a lesson in God's dealing with human beings. These are people with a ministry, who can teach us something of what it means to be called to develop one's gift.

I believe each one of us has at least one gift. It may not be so obvious, or public, as writing books. It may be a gift for friendship, or loving children, or teaching, or leadership, or administration.

Each of us must discern God's "call" on our own life and faithfully develop our gift for the glory of God and the furthering of his kingdom. As you read the stories of these authors, you will learn more about God's ways with his people. You will see the diversity, and unity, of their vision for their ministry. You will discover what makes your favorite authors tick, and you will read about their sometimes passionate perspectives on faith, calling, and fiction.

No matter what it is God has equipped *you* to do for him, these stories will point you to the underlying universal principles of fulfilling that calling. I have arranged their stories in sections that indicate some aspect of calling, more or less reflecting the order in which God's direction is experienced.

Though not every fine Christian novelist is represented here, the authors I have included articulate what many of us feel but can't put words to. Listen as these "wise ones" tell their stories and open their hearts. Your own heart won't be the same.

CHAPTER 1

Say Yes to God

"Every choice moves us closer to or farther away from something.

Where are your choices taking your life? What do your behaviors

demonstrate that you are saying yes or no to in life?"

— ERIC ALLENBAUGH

"My intent is to use story the way Christ used parables: to find something eternal that needs to be said, then wrap it up in enough entertainment so the reader will continue turning the pages as he or she is drawn closer to the heart of God."

BILL MYERS is a prolific film director and author. His films and books have won more than forty awards, including three New York International Film Festival Awards and the CS Lewis Honor Book Award. He cocreated the popular McGee and Me! children's video series, some of which were aired on ABC as Weekend Specials. He's written several children's book series including BLOODHOUNDS, INC., INCREDIBLE WORLDS OF WALLY MCDOOGLE, FORBIDDEN DOORS, and MCGEE AND ME! He is also author of several nonfiction books and the bestselling adult novels *Blood of Heaven, Threshold, Fire of Heaven,* and *Eli.*

Just Say Yes

If you'd asked the teenage Bill Myers what he wanted to be when he grew up, he would have readily told you, "A dentist." It seemed like a respectable, mature type of profession to which to aspire. But God had other plans.

During those same teenage years, Bill thought Christianity was boring. He knew what John 10:10 said ("I have come that they may have life, and have it to the full"), but it wasn't true in his life. His brother Dale, nine years older, had an explanation: "The reason you're bored is because you're only half a Christian."

That made Bill angry. "What do you mean, 'half a Christian'?" he asked.

Dale said, "You've got Jesus down as Savior, but you don't know anything about him being your boss."

"What's that got to do with being bored?"

Dale replied, "I'll make you a promise. If you promise never to say no to God, regardless of how ignorant you think he is or uninformed he may be of the situation, your life will become anything but boring."

Bill figured he'd give it a shot.

When Bill started his freshman year at the University of Washington, he had seen three motion pictures in his life: *Pollyanna, Mary Poppins,* and *The Parent Trap.* ("I grew up in the Cascade Mountains in a mountain hamlet—one stoplight in town," he explains.) Then he saw *The Godfather.*

"I wandered around the campus for several days, numb," he recalls. He began a dialogue with God: "God, you've got to raise people up in communications. Film is so powerful, and look how it's being used!" A resonating impression nagged at him; he brushed it

13

aside. "Come on, get serious," he continued. "I'm saying you've got to raise up people who are film directors and people in communications, to combat this kind of stuff. . . . Knock it off, God! I'm trying to carry on a conversation here." But the impression kept building and building, until finally Bill gave in: "It became real clear he wanted me to be a part of what I was praying for."

Bill changed his major to film directing. One problem, though: the University of Washington didn't have a film directing department, or even a film department of any kind. Bill switched to a small college, the only college he could find in western Washington that had a film department, and immediately discovered that the film majors were going to Rome, Italy, to study for a year.

"Sorry, we're all booked up," he was told. "Besides, you don't know anything about film." (Which was true, Bill admits.) But he kept saying, "I understand that, but I'm going." And, as God's ways would have it, one of the students didn't have the money to go, so Bill took his place. (Turns out the student was Matt Groening, who later created *The Simpsons*.) Within six weeks, Bill Myers was in Rome, studying a subject he knew nothing about, in a language he couldn't speak.

"To understand how foolish this was, you have to understand how hopeless I am with language," Bill says. "It took me a long time even to learn to speak as a child, and I was impossible with language. To get into college, I had to take two years of a foreign language. I devised all kinds of ingenious ways to cheat my way through French class. I told God, 'This is the epitome of foolishness, to be studying film in Rome, Italy.'" Yet, there he was. He'd made his promise, and God had taken him to Rome, Italy, to study film.

Bill graduated and moved to Los Angeles to become a rich and famous film director—and discovered there were already plenty of those to go around. He turned to acting, but the sporadic jobs didn't pay the bills. Bill told the Lord, "Maybe I made a mistake about this film stuff. But I think after my year of working hard in Rome, I can do just about anything in film making—except, of course, write." He was thinking of his communication problem and the C's and D's he had earned in his one writing class in college. "But," he continued his prayer, "I agreed always to say yes to you, so even if you were 'foolish' enough to want me to do something like that, I'd be open."

About six weeks later Bill was directing a stage play in Hollywood. Out of the blue, a television producer came up to him and said, "Bill, will you write an episode for a TV series?" Though Bill had never thought he could do that, they were paying and he was starving, so the answer seemed clear.

"I wrote the world's worst TV show," Bill says. "It was so bad. The only time I threw something at the TV was at my own show. But I figured I would keep writing, since someone was paying me." Bill wrote two more TV shows, both of which, he says, "they had the good foresight not to produce. But I was getting my own little private writing course. As you keep writing and writing, you hope you become less inept at it."

Some time later he got a call from an editor of a Christian publishing house who had heard there was a "famous Christian TV writer" living on the West Coast, and wouldn't it be a keen idea if they could get him to write some books for them. Bill asked the telling question, "Do you pay?" They said yes, and so did he.

"So I wrote the world's worst book," Bill says. Then he wrote another, and another. "I felt totally inept and unqualified to do any of these things. It's one thing to write a TV script, which is basically telling a movie you see in your head. It's another thing to sit down and write a book—I mean, that's what *writers* do."

But God had prepared him even for this. Bill had been teaching Bible studies in his home, and now he was being asked to write Bible commentary. Bill says, "Though it was frightening, in a way God eased me into it. Yes, he made me come up to the plate, but he let me take baby steps. Writing the commentaries was what I was doing anyway in the Bible studies, only instead of talking I was writing it down."

That became God's pattern with Bill: each time, the next step was almost like the first one. "God easing me into the water until I was over my head without knowing it." Once he was writing, he told God, "I guess I made a mistake again. I guess you want me to do anything *but* direct films." Again, six weeks later, he got a call to direct his first film—which won an award. Other films followed. The first novel he wrote was based on the film he'd already written. Again, God eased him into something he felt totally unqualified to do. "The key to my success is I'm a loser, and I knew it a lot sooner than anyone else," Bill says. "I know if I did it my way I'd just mess up, so I let God do it his way. I never say no to God."

Bill says his role model in Scripture is not Joseph or Paul or Peter or David. Rather, it's Balaam's donkey. "People laugh when I say this," Bill says, "but I'm quite serious." Balaam's donkey saw the angel of the Lord, and it was terrified and got out of the Lord's way. "That's what I do. I'm really just a coward at heart. I've learned if you get out of the way and let God do it his way—if you die to self— then it's amazing what he can do. He made Balaam's donkey speak!"

Bill says the best example of this—a microcosm of his whole life—is how McGee and Me!, the children's video series, came to be. One day Bill got a call from someone who said, "We've got a million dollars. Can you help us spend it?"

"I took that to the Lord in prayer for about half a second," Bill chuckles, "and had a clear divine epiphany. I said, 'Absolutely!' "

"Good. We're getting together eighteen of the most creative Christians in the country for a weekend at the Ritz-Carlton in Laguna Niguel, and we're going to create a Christian TV and video series for kids that's going to be great," Bill was told.

Bill went down to the fancy resort at Laguna Niguel—and felt completely out of his element. "I did not fit in there at all," he says. "These guys had written for *Happy Days* and marketed Amy Grant. I had *seen* a few episodes of *Happy Days* and owned a *CD* of Amy Grant." Bill says he embarrassed himself so much the first night, he retired to his room and had a good self-pity cry in his room. He told the Lord, "I know I agreed never to say no to you, but this is way beyond my reach. I'm making a total idiot of myself." He devised a way to cut God a deal and still be true to his word: "God, I've got one lame idea about a kid with an imaginary cartoon-type friend. I'll share that with the group, and then I'll make up some excuse so I can go home. I'm wasting this ministry's money, and it would be better if I just left."

The next morning Bill went downstairs to what he intended to be his last meeting. He shared his vague kernel of an idea. The group pressed him for more. "I was winging it, making things up as I went, trying to get out the door, trying to say I gotta go." This went on throughout the weekend. On Sunday night, Bill went for a walk with executive producer Dan Johnson, "the man with the check." Dan said, "Bill, it's become very apparent to us that you're the man God has called to quarterback this new series."

Inside, Bill was thinking, *Here we go again.* He managed to calmly say, "Of course, that makes all the sense in the world." And so Bill Myers and Ken Johnson, his partner who had a background in animation, created the successful McGee and Me! series. But it was pure reliance on God all the way. "Ken and I would look at each other, terrified, because there was a million dollars riding on this project. One or the other of us would say, 'Balaam's donkey?' and the other would nod and then we'd get to work."

In the world's eyes, Bill is a success. But he insists that the key to his success is a profound realization of his own ineptness. "The key to my success is I'm a loser, a coward, a wimp, a crybaby. I'm co-dependent and co-everything, but it doesn't matter, because 'I' am dead." Galatians 2:20 ("I have been crucified with Christ and I no longer live, but Christ lives in me. The life I live in the body, I live by faith in the Son of God, who loved me and gave himself for me") is not just a nice verse to Bill; it's a summation of the only way he knows to live the Christian life and discover God's calling. Convinced of his own ineptness, he's thrown himself into total reliance on God instead of his own abilities.

God has taken that dependence and pushed Bill into adventures he'd never have dreamed would be his. "As a film director, I've been lost in the rain forests of South America, chased by giraffes in

Africa, had knives pulled on me in inner cities. I've even had Muslims try to kill me." Hardly a boring life! "My life is so incredibly overflowing," Bill says, "because I learned very early to quit doing it my way. This business of always saying yes to God is remarkable. And that's why if I'm enjoying any success for this season of time, it's simply because I quit trying to be a dentist!"

Not that a dentist who's sold out to God would have any less boring a life, he would hasten to add. He once gave his testimony to a group in Pennsylvania, and a coal miner came up to him afterward and said, "Bill, I made that same promise to the Lord, and I got to tell you, my life is nothing like yours." Bill thought, *Oh really? There goes my three-part speech!* But he invited the man out to lunch to talk more.

Over hamburgers, Bill invited the coal miner to tell him about his life. He said, "I made that same commitment never to say no to God, and I'm not traveling the world and directing films or any of that stuff."

"Well, what are you doing?" Bill asked.

He said, "My life's been pretty dull . . . though there was that time a big fight broke out between management and all the workers, and since management and all the workers kind of liked me, I was able to step in between them and stop the fight and defuse the situation. That was pretty interesting."

"Uh, very interesting," Bill said. "Anything else?"

"Well, yes. There was the time McPherson had the gun to his mouth, and his family was in front of him, and he was on the phone, calling me up, and I talked him out of killing himself."

As the two men talked on, it became apparent that, indeed, this coal miner's life was just as exciting in its own way as Bill's was. By the time they were done with lunch, the miner said with a grin, "Yeah, it is a pretty cool life!"

"What would happen," Bill asks, "if every Christian would do this? What would happen if each one of us would set aside our own agenda and decide to always say yes to doing it God's way—and affirmed that every day? Most of us give God seventy or eighty percent and don't trust him with that last twenty percent. If we could really believe that God loves us completely, and we are great in his eyes—if we didn't have to spend our energy proving our own worth—then we'd be free to let him make us great in his eyes. I mean it when I say the only reason God calls on me is because I've made myself available. It's like God's looking around the classroom for people who have their hands raised, and I've got mine up, so he says, 'Okay, Bill.' It seems there are so few who are willing to do it totally God's way, that anyone who is willing is sure to be called on."

Bill told his wife that when he dies, he doesn't want any Bible verses or epitaphs on his tombstone. Instead, he wants a picture of him jumping off a cliff, yelling, "Here we go again!"

"That's what my whole life has been, jumping off one cliff after another, simply because I promised to always say yes, never to say no to God."

Are you ready for the adventure of your life? Then just say yes to God!

SHARON EWELL FOSTER is a regular contributor to *Daily Guideposts.* Her first novel, *Passing by Samaria,* became a bestseller and was a Christy Award 2001 finalist in two categories; it won for New Novel. Her second book, *Ain't No River,* released to critical acclaim. Her most recent novel is *Riding Through Shadows.*

"Through fiction I am able, with the help of the Lord, to help people discover and see Bible truth and live truer lives by translating that truth into their everyday lives."

The Other Side of Fear

Though Sharon Foster was always "a reading machine" who longed to be a writer, she spent the first thirty-seven years of her life skirting the writing issue. She came close a couple of times—she worked as a technical writer for a while and at another point wrote a news column. But though she felt deep inside that she was called to write, she was afraid to answer that call.

The obstacles were great: She was a single mother with two children to support. She had a wonderful job as an instructor in charge of the faculty development branch at a military base; she trained military journalists and broadcasters how to teach their subject matter to others who would learn their specialty. "It was a wonderful job—secure, interesting," Sharon says. "I was good at it. Sometimes I could feel the Lord's power as I was teaching. I was able to talk about Christian things without preaching to them. I thought it was wonderful that I was ministering to these tough military people, touching their hearts so much that sometimes they would come up and hug me afterward. Yes, I was digging where I was."

Yet still some nagging voice told Sharon she should be writing. Once her young son told her, "If you would just write, we wouldn't have to suffer." Though she was making good money, tithing to the church, and living carefully, she found it difficult to make ends meet. Both her son—he was nine years old when he said this—and her older daughter kept telling her she should write, as did friends. But it didn't add up. How could she write and support her family?

Finally, she opened the door a crack. She promised the Lord she would get up at five every morning faithfully and write, if he would show her what to do. "I thought I would write something, nothing would come of it, and I could tell the Lord, 'See, I tried,' " Sharon says. So she got up early and wrote, sometimes just, "I don't know why I'm writing. . . ."

She also did some homework. She picked up a copy of *Writer's Digest* and found a blurb in the back saying that Questar was looking for Christian romances about minorities. Well, it was a direction anyway. She went to her local Christian bookstore to look for fiction published by Questar. "At the time, I didn't even know that Christian fiction existed; I had to ask where the fiction aisle was. I was raised in a Christian home, but only visited the Christian bookstore looking for Bibles or nonfiction."

She began by writing longhand in a steno notebook. Then a friend smuggled her a word processor from her packrat husband's cache of broken computers. Sharon faithfully worked every morning on her story, writing scenes that played out before her mind like a movie, not knowing at all where the story was going.

She received a brochure about the Sandy Cove Christian Writers Conference. When she saw it cost ninety-five dollars, she threw the brochure away.

Nevertheless, she felt God wanted her to go. So she prayed, "Okay, Lord, if you want me to go, you come up with the money." She had sixty-five dollars. When her mother unexpectedly sent her a check for thirty-five dollars, she figured she'd gotten her answer. She would go for one day, the very last day of the conference.

Driving to the conference, she listened to a tape by Joyce Meyers about finding and fulfilling one's destiny. She was almost embarrassed to have anyone look at her coffee- and jam-stained manuscript, but she told herself what she always told her students: Never be afraid to get feedback; it will help you develop. "I'm just looking for feedback," she told herself.

When she got there she felt lost, but Denise Williamson, an author who was on the conference staff, took Sharon under her wing. Sharon told Deni about how she came to be at the conference and added, "I'm not ready to see an editor yet; I only have three chapters." Deni said that there was an editor from Multnomah, formerly Questar, the publisher that was looking for the kind of fiction

Sharon had begun to write. "Probably too late to make an appointment," Sharon told herself, but she checked anyway. Sure enough, all the slots were filled to see the editor, Karen Ball, but there *was* a line through one name. Sharon wrote her name in at that appointment slot. "I figured Karen could always tell me to go away if she couldn't see anyone," Sharon says.

Sharon met with magazine editors, who were all very encouraging about her work, but Sharon figured they were just being nice Christian people. She entered the large dining room to meet with Karen Ball and found the Multnomah table. Sharon handed Karen her manuscript and told her she was trying to write a romance. Karen began reading and said, "This is not a romance." Sharon thought, *If I could just crawl out of this room right now I might survive.* But then Karen said, her voice growing louder, "This isn't a romance, it's *To Kill a Mockingbird!*"

An agent came over and asked Sharon if she would consider her as an agent. "The whole day sort of exploded and turned crazy," Sharon says. Karen took the rest of the manuscript to read. People whispered about her: "That's the one that editor was all excited about."

Sharon had a headache and wasn't planning on staying for the awards ceremony after the dinner on that last night, but Karen strongly urged her to stay. No one was more amazed than Sharon when her name was called as winner of the Alpha Award for "most promising new author."

"It was all like a dream," Sharon says. Within two weeks she signed with an agent who "doesn't take on new writers," and a few weeks after that she signed a contract to write two books. All on the strength of the three chapters she had written in obedience to God's calling her to begin writing. None of it seemed real yet.

Sharon just kept writing, even though she wasn't sure where the story was going. She had no big picture. She just wrote the scenes that came to her after she had prayed diligently for the ability to write what God wanted her to write. It was like writing pieces to a jigsaw puzzle; each day she came up with a piece, but she didn't know how the pieces fit together.

Then one day a phrase came to her: "passing by Samaria." She thought it must be a title to a movie or something. She did a search and studied every reference to Samaria in the Bible. Sharon meditated on what such a phrase might mean, thinking about the verse in Acts 1:8. She explains, "Jesus told his followers to witness about him in Jerusalem, Judea, and Samaria, and the ends of the earth. I thought of how Jerusalem is like our personal relationship with God and ourselves and our families, Judea is like the people we grow up with who are like us, and Samaria represents the people who live amongst us that we're not sure we want to love and reconcile with. We'd rather 'pass by' Samaria and those people. I thought, *God, that's great. I should put that in a book sometime. But it wouldn't be easy for people to receive, so I'd have to couch it in something else, like fiction. . . .* Then it occurred to me, that's what the book I was writing was all about!" Suddenly the jigsaw puzzle came into focus, and she saw how the pieces fit together. The title stuck, and her first book was *Passing by Samaria.*

That book was written mostly in those early morning sessions. God had opened the doors wide for Sharon, but still she was reluctant to go all the way through them. She felt God urging her to quit her job to write full time. She was afraid to do it. God had been providing for her all the way—for instance, someone she had spoken to at a Christian conference sent her a computer in the mail—but still she was afraid to give up the security of her job. She knew how to teach; she wasn't sure she knew how to write. She approached her children, secretly hoping they would protest her quitting, but they both said, "You should do what you think God is telling you to do."

During that time of wrestling over her job, she sat at a Christian conference and suddenly found herself weeping. At first she didn't know why, then she knew for certain God was asking her to leave her job. She talked to a woman who was also a writer. The other writer said that she knew women who wrote full time, but they all had husbands to help them. She said, "What I admire are the men who have families who make the commitment to write and step out in faith."

That struck Sharon. Stepping out in faith. Wasn't that what God was asking her to do? It felt more like he was asking her to dive into twelve feet of water and start swimming! But hadn't she just been reading Isaiah 54:5, about how her husband is her Maker, the mighty Lord of hosts, the God of all the earth? Wouldn't he take care of her?

So she stepped out in faith. She handed in her resignation. Now the Lord was truly her employer, truly the one paying her salary.

Shortly after she resigned from her job, she got word that Kweisi Mfume, the president of the NAACP, was going to endorse *Passing by Samaria.* "I had sent him a copy of the manuscript, sure he wouldn't even consider endorsing it," she says. But she sent it anyway, and God opened another door.

Her publisher, Multnomah Press, worked with the NAACP to sponsor a Follow Your Dream essay contest, and Sharon judged the contest and went to the NAACP convention to give the winners their prizes. Her book hit the bestseller list within a few months of being published—almost unheard of for a first-time novelist. She speaks at churches and conferences, and doors are opening right and left. She's working on more novels and writing devotionals for *Guideposts.*

Though it feels as if she has dived into twelve feet of water, Sharon says she knows that the difference between swimming in six feet of water and swimming in twelve feet is all psychological. Feeling like she's in over her head just keeps her dependent on God— a place God wants all of us to be. She feels that God is now using every single experience she's ever had to equip her to fulfill her call, from the books she read that taught her what good writing is, to the job she was so afraid to leave that has equipped her to speak and teach. It took Sharon a long time to finally answer the call to write, but God used everything in the meantime to bring her to the place of effectiveness she is at now. Doors are opening, people are telling her that her books are changing their lives, and opportunities to write and speak are keeping her busy and providing for the needs of her family.

In pondering her story, Sharon thinks of the parable of the Prodigal Son. The son wanted his inheritance early, and he wanted to use it for his own purposes instead of his father's. Sharon says that God gives each of us gifts, and using them for purposes other than his is tantamount to squandering them, as the Prodigal Son did. But God is an ever-patient Father, waiting every day for his wayward children to come back to him. He waited thirty-seven years for Sharon to finally heed his call. And then he welcomed her with wide open arms and poured out the blessings of confirmation upon her, just as the father of the Prodigal Son had a party to celebrate his homecoming.

If you have felt there is something God wants you to do, but you have held back in fear, take heart. You haven't missed your chance entirely; God is certainly able to open doors of opportunity you've never dreamed existed. Take one small step in the direction you feel drawn to go, as Sharon did when she got up early to write. Trust that God will open the right doors at the right time. Trust that he waits to hear your answer with arms wide open to enfold you.

On the other side of fear great blessing awaits. Nothing can match the sense of awe in watching God fit you into his great plans for the world.

RANDY ALCORN

"*My calling is to probe beneath the surface into the deep longings of people, then to open a door into the invisible spiritual realm so people can see ultimate realities—including God, angels, demons, heaven, and hell—with the eyes of faith and imagination. You can't help but live differently once you learn to see differently.*"

RANDY ALCORN is the author of more than fifteen nonfiction books and novels, several of which regularly show up on the bestseller list. He directs Eternal Perspective Ministries *(www.epm.org)*, in which his writing and speaking "teach the principles of God's Word, emphasizing an eternal viewpoint," and other ministries "reach the needy in Christ's name." EPM seeks to meet a variety of physical, social, emotional, intellectual, and spiritual needs. Randy's calling goes beyond writing, and his books are the foundation of a larger ministry.

A Matter of Perspective

Randy Alcorn's life, calling, and ministry can be rolled up in one word: perspective.

As a boy, Randy used to gaze into the heavens through the telescope his parents gave him. He vividly remembers gazing out at the stars one clear night, pondering that the great galaxy of Andromeda was millions of light-years away. It was all so big, so vast . . . he started crying. "It's not a typical thing for a tough sixth-grade boy to look up at the stars and cry. But I felt such awe—and emptiness."

At the time he was reading comic books and science fiction, anything that stimulated his imagination. Even at that age he felt a stirring in his heart, a longing for something larger than himself. His folks were not Christians, and he didn't know what to name or do with these longings. Not until high school.

That's when he met a Christian girl. She lived fourteen miles away from Randy's home but would come to his area to attend a church youth group. Someone invited Randy, too. "At first I went so I could see her," he confesses. "But once I was there I was interested in what was said. I heard the gospel, read the Bible on my own, went to church even when she wasn't going to be there. One day I was reading the Bible and realized I was believing it. I got down on my knees and gave my life to Christ."

The youth pastor gave Randy a key to his office and said he could read whatever he found on the shelves. Thus began Randy's love for Christian books. He was especially influenced by C. S. Lewis—an influence that continues today. In fact, he says that he's never written a book, fiction or nonfiction, in which he hasn't been influenced by Lewis in some way. His recent bestseller, *Lord Foulgrin's Letters*, was inspired by Lewis's *Screwtape Letters*; in *Deadline*,

Lewis's *Mere Christianity* plays a pivotal role. In his novel *Dominion*, C. S. Lewis is actually a minor character.

Randy remembers pulling out his telescope some time after he became a Christian. This time when he gazed up at the stars, he felt something else. The awe was still there, but it wasn't empty. He now knew the Creator and Savior who made all that vastness for his glory. What a different perspective! "I cried again, but for a very different reason. Now I was inside the circle; now I knew the God who created all this," he says. Thoughtfully, he adds, "All Christians are inside the circle, but sometimes we forget and live our lives as though we were on the outside. We sometimes forget that we were made for a person—Jesus—and a place—heaven. No other person and no other place can satisfy our deepest longings."

Randy attended Multnomah Bible College and Western Baptist Seminary, earning his Th.B. and M.A. in biblical studies. He became a pastor and, alongside Stu Weber, led a church in Boring, Oregon. Within fourteen years the church grew to two thousand members. While the church was thriving on the outside, Randy was burdened by the number of Christians devastated by sexual immorality. He started writing a book addressing this huge problem and approached a publisher about it.

The first of two key life-changing events happened in 1985. In the same month that his first book, *Christians in the Wake of the Sexual Revolution*, was published, Randy was diagnosed with insulin-dependent diabetes. "God used this to remind me of my dependence on him, in a daily, concrete way," Randy says. "Before that, I knew intellectually that I was dependent on God for every breath. But I was really very independent and self-sufficient. Now I have a built-in reminder every single day when I take my five or six blood tests and insulin injections: 'Apart from me you can do nothing' (John 15:5b). The timing was perfect. Of all the months in my life when I could have gotten a serious disease it happened in the one month when my first book was published. That was a reminder that my writing isn't about me, it's about the Lord, and without his strength it will accomplish nothing."

His disease brought a major change of focus—again, perspective. Randy's life verse became 2 Corinthians 4:18: "So we fix our eyes not on what is seen, but on what is unseen. For what is seen is temporary, but what is unseen is eternal."

The second life-changing event—the one that launched his current ministry—seemed like anything but a gift at the time. Because Randy Alcorn believes in living, not just discussing, his convictions, he had been involved in pro-life activities. He'd been on the board of the first Crisis Pregnancy Center in his city. He and his wife had opened their home to a pregnant girl, who came to Christ while she lived with them. Randy had also been involved in peaceful, nonviolent civil disobedience, standing in front of the doors of abortion clinics to intervene for unborn children, trying to convince parents not to kill their babies.

The abortion clinic sued him and others. In the judgment against him, he was ordered to compensate the clinic for the income it lost due to abortions prevented by his presence. Randy told the judge, "I will pay anyone money I owe them, but I will not write out a check to an abortion clinic, because they'll use it to keep killing babies."

Randy's church then received a writ of garnishment, ordering them to pay a portion of Randy's monthly wages to the abortion clinic. "The only way around that," Randy says, "was to resign, so the church didn't owe me any money. It was heartbreaking—I loved being a pastor, I loved my church, and I didn't envision myself leaving. But the Lord providentially yanked me out of that position, and it ended up being a great blessing. It was just like Genesis 50 and what Joseph said to his brothers—the abortion clinic intended it for evil, but God intended it for good."

One great good that emerged was the birth of Eternal Perspective Ministries. "When I had to figure out what to do," Randy says, "I thought, I have a love for missions, pro-life work, and writing, and I enjoy teaching and speaking. How can I wrap those all together into one ministry? So my family and I started EPM and did the exact things the Lord laid on our hearts." So his calling was refocused, deepened, and confirmed.

One of the great blessings of starting this ministry was that Randy was suddenly free to write much more. Before, as a pastor, it had been a continual challenge to carve out the time to write. He had refused to write on church time and periodically asked for unpaid leaves of absence to devote to writing. Now, in his new ministry, he is free to write as much as he wants, as part of his ministry job description. Writing is not the end for Randy, but the means to his primary calling—to point people toward an eternal perspective. His goal is to change people's minds and hearts, through whatever communication means he can: books—both fiction and nonfiction, speaking, a quarterly newsletter, his Web site. He is free to continue his pro-life activities. And he doesn't give a dime of God's money to anything his conscience can't support.

Because it can't be garnished, Randy receives minimum wage for his salary. Ninety percent of what comes in to EPM through his book royalties is given away to missions and the pro-life cause; ten percent goes into the general fund, which is also supported by loyal givers to the nonprofit ministry. This covers the overhead to run EPM, including the salaries of Randy, his wife, and three part-time staffers. Randy had followed the advice of his book *Money, Possessions and Eternity* about living debt-free. In fact, he had to resign from the church just two months after he mailed in his last mortgage check.

Randy says his books have a double impact: Not only do the messages contained in them touch people's lives, but the income they generate supports what God is doing through strategic ministries. "It's a setup I never could have come up with on my own," Randy says in wonder. "God had to yank me out of a ministry I loved to create something entirely unique, of his doing."

Randy's books have earned more money than most writers dream of. Yet none of the money goes to him—it all goes to the ministry. It gives Randy a tremendous freedom, he says. "Greed is kept in check, because my lifestyle doesn't go up if a book commands a greater advance or higher royalties. It's just more money for the work of the ministry." When he sees his books on the best-seller list, he figures, "Maybe the Lord wanted more money for missions work."

Randy Alcorn demonstrates that when you "seek first the kingdom of God and his righteousness," temporal needs will be met. In more direct and obvious ways than the rest of us, Randy depends on God for every need. For his life and breath, as his diabetes reminds him. For every temporal need to be met, as he lives on a restricted wage. And for spiritual strength and perspective, as he wrestles with daily priorities and the responsibilities of his ministry.

Yet don't all of us work for the Lord, directly or indirectly? Aren't we all dependent on God's grace for every breath and temporal need? Aren't we all called to submit our talents to God for his use? Aren't we all required to obediently seek justice and mercy and tell others of the grace of God? Don't we all struggle to keep our priorities focused on what really matters? In whatever circumstance we find ourselves, we are called to the same kind of obedience and dependence Randy demonstrates.

Randy Alcorn's story shows how radical dependence triggers God's absolute faithfulness and a thrilling creativity. God has opened doors for all of Randy's passions to be expressed. He has circumvented a court judgment and provided a way for Randy's gifts to be used to make money for God's own work. Randy's books have sold well, not to make Randy rich but to provide for God's work. And God continues to extend his message of grace and eternity through a ministry that clearly he called into being.

What amazing things might God do through your radical dependence and obedience? The only way to find out is to set your sights on eternity, on the unseen, give God your all, and watch for the miracles.

CHAPTER 2

Uniquely Gifted

"The work of art which I do not make, none other will ever make."

— SIMONE WEIL

"Human beings ought to communicate and share all the gifts they have received from God."

—MEISTER ECKHART

JIM WALKER

JIM WALKER'S first published book was a nonfiction bestseller (*Husbands Who Won't Lead and Wives Who Won't Follow*), but fiction is his first love. With Bethany House, he published the eight-volume WELLS FARGO TRAIL series. In 1998, his first book in the MYSTERIES IN TIME SERIES, *Murder on the Titanic*, came out and became number one on Amazon.com's list for 1998.

"In my books, you have to read underneath the story line or you will miss the point. I think that's the way it should be. When Jesus told parables, he didn't explain what they meant. He told stories to make a point, to get people to think about what the story meant and how it affected their own lives. I want my readers to think deeply, to ask themselves how they would deal with the situations the characters face, and why they would do it that way."

Obedient to God's Design

Jim Walker defines his calling as a storyteller. He can't remember a time when he wasn't telling stories in one form or another. One of his earliest memories is of going to the barbershop with his dad when he was four or five years old. He sat in the barber chair and told a story of a purple horse that had made its way through the pasture. Weaving a story that would entertain others thrilled him. It was what he was designed to do. It was as if he couldn't keep from doing it.

Yet one blatant obstacle interfered: Jim Walker had a stutter. From early childhood on, he would stumble over certain sounds. His dilemma was acute: on the one hand he was driven to express himself clearly and gain a response from people. On the other hand, whenever he opened his mouth, he could never be sure the words would come out right. He lived "alert all the time" to things and people around him. "I never knew when a teacher would call on me, and I would know what to say but just couldn't get it out right," he says. "Though it was difficult, in one way it was a blessing. It caused me to make sure that whenever I said something, it made an impact."

But inside, the young Jim struggled. Why did God create him with this great longing to express himself verbally, yet at that same time allow that expression to be so difficult? At the time, he had no answer. But God did.

In eighth grade, one of his teachers urged him to take a public speaking class. "I didn't want to, but I did," Jim says. "It was very good for me. I had to practice speaking in front of a mirror." Faithful practice helped Jim overcome his stutter. He won awards, placing first in the whole state of California for impromptu speaking as a junior in high school and first in extemporaneous speaking in his senior year. The awards validated that at his very core, he was designed to be a communicator.

"God's design is absolutely perfect," he says. He believes now that even the obstacles are part of God's plan. "It's as if God says, 'I really want it this way, even if it seems like an obstacle to you. I have something I want to do in your life [through the obstacle], and if you will just let me I will be happy to do it.' We live our lives and allow God to work in us in a very miraculous and wonderful way."

The wonder was that Jim never lacked for a venue in which to use his gift for expression. When he joined the Air Force, he, along with thousands of others, decided to sign up to work in the survival school. But he was chosen. His job teaching survival training for the Air Force involved lots of storytelling. Later he taught speech and history, coached football, pastored a church, and worked for a parachurch organization. Storytelling was an integral part of each of these occupations. "It's the thread that weaves its way through everything I've ever thought or done; it's what identifies who I am," Jim says. "A person's calling ought to be that identifying trait, the thing that makes you what you are. If you want to know what God designed you to do, look at what you're doing when you shine." Therein is the key to your calling or unique mission in life.

For Jim, writing is simply one additional expression of the way God designed him. His first book arose from a series of sermon topics on marital roles and leadership in the Christian marriage. Someone told him the series would make a great book. Jim realized there was nothing written on this particular aspect of marriage— and so did the publishers he contacted with his proposal. He wrote *Husbands Who Won't Lead and Wives Who Won't Follow.*

But his interest in fiction was growing at the same time. His professors in seminary had tried to get him interested in Louis L'Amour, but he didn't have time to read anything beyond his class assignments. When he finally picked up a L'Amour book, he was skeptical. "I picked up *Last Breed*, which dealt with a flyer who went down over the bleakest part of Russia. I thought, *This is what I taught in the Air Force—survival skills.* I was amazed at how accurate and what a good yarn it was." Jim went on to read more books by Louis L'Amour, and at some point he thought, *Maybe I could do this.*

His first novels were westerns. In the WELLS FARGO TRAIL series, Jim delves deeply into the heart of the main character, a man who is cold and unapproachable. The novels track the main character's journey into intimacy with others and a deep knowledge of God. They are good books to give to nonbelievers who like westerns, because they are not preachy and the main character's spiritual journey unfolds as the series progresses. In fact, four of the novels in this series were nominated for Best Western Novel by the Western Writers of America, a group that traditionally shuns all Christian publications.

Jim also wrote murder mysteries. *Murder on the Titanic* was a combination of good writing and excellent timing (it came out two weeks after the movie *Titanic* was released). Jim's storytelling gifts were being validated by the world.

But even if the world doesn't validate the gift, at least for a time, Jim feels it's important to continue to express it. The joy comes in using the gift God gave you. Jim loves the whole process involved in writing a book. Researching is downright fun ("If I'm writing about a particular place, I'll go there so I can experience firsthand what it's like to sleep on the ground there or raft on the river or explore the cave"). Reading about an era, interviewing people, creating characters, and crafting scenes—all this is fulfilling in itself. Whether his books sell a lot or a little, Jim feels his first responsibility is to write the kind of stories he feels God has gifted him to write. If for some reason he couldn't write the kind of stories he wants to tell, he says he'd just find some other way to express himself. "If I wasn't writing books, I'd be telling stories to the homeless or something. I can't help it," he says. "I have to be obedient to God's design."

"Obedient to God's design." Have you realized that God's will for you is inextricably tied to the thing that you do almost as naturally as breathing, the one thread that weaves through your life, the thing you can't help doing? For Jim, it's telling stories. Maybe for you it's organizing things, or evoking a response in people, or making things, or solving conflicts between people. Whatever your gift is, the world needs it. It's your particular light, not meant to be hidden under a basket. If you don't know what it is, pray for God to show you. Look at the things you have loved doing, especially in childhood.

The key to your contribution to life, to God's kingdom, is in the way he designed you. In obedience to that design, you will find great joy.

ROBIN JONES GUNN

"The banner over my life is the conviction that God is the relentless Lover and we are his first love, and he never gives up on us. This is the theme that comes up in all my books."

ROBIN JONES GUNN grew up in southern California and began writing for publication seventeen years ago, when her children were young. Along with writing fourteen books for children, Robin has also written over sixty articles and several gift books. Her storytelling attention turned to writing novels for teens since she and her husband, Ross, have been involved in full-time youth ministry for more than twenty years. Her twelve-book CHRISTY MILLER SERIES was followed by the twelve-book SIERRA JENSEN SERIES. As Robin's audience of teen readers grew, she began writing THE GLENBROOKE SERIES. She is also completing five more novels to continue the story of Christy Miller and her friends.

Robin and her family make their home near Portland, Oregon.

Reaching "Teens in the Tent"

R obin Jones Gunn didn't dream of being a writer. She thought she'd be a missionary. As a teenager, she went to the Urbana missionary convention and got a printout of possible missionary positions from around the world. She applied for an opening as a laundry supervisor in Kenya, but then learned the position was already filled. "I remember feeling, 'I can't even serve God washing clothes on the mission field,' " she says.

God had other plans for her—a different mission field to reach, using different gifts. Robin did hear a clear "call," but it came from a very unexpected source.

Her husband, Ross, is a full-time youth pastor, and Robin worked alongside him. In 1986 they took the youth to the beach on a camping trip. Robin noticed that all the girls were in the tent reading a stack of books they had brought from the library. "Why are you in here when you could be out on the beach?" Robin asked incredulously.

"We'd rather do this," they replied.

Curious as to what was so engrossing, Robin asked the girls to pick out three of their favorites so she could read them, too. Robin skimmed the books and then asked if their parents knew what they were reading. "This is not the sort of thing I would like to see you fill your minds with," she told them.

"Then you give us something to read," they said.

Robin went to the Christian bookstore in search of books suitable for teenage girls. "The only Christian fiction out at that time was by Janette Oke," she recalls. Robin bought every Oke book she found and gave them to the girls on Sunday.

By Wednesday they had read them all. They asked for more.

Robin told them, "That's all there is."

"Then you write one," they said.

Up to that point, Robin had written a number of children's books. She had started when her own two children were young. That was a hobby, but this was a call.

You write one, the girls in the tent had challenged. The words echoed deep within Robin.

"But I don't know if I can write books for teenagers," she told the girls.

"We'll tell you what to write," they told her. "We'll tell you what is interesting to us."

Robin answered the challenge. She started writing *Summer Promise* and took each chapter to the girls, who told her what worked and what didn't. For two years Robin labored over that first book.

Then she tried to sell it to a publisher. Ten publishers turned it down. "There just isn't a market for this sort of thing," they all said.

Robin knew otherwise. She knew that all across America, not just in California where she lived, teenage girls were huddling in their tents or their bedrooms devouring the novels they got from the library. She wanted to shout, "There is a market! You just can't see them because they're in the tent!"

"I was almost ready to give up," Robin admits.

Then she came across Jeremiah 20:9, where Jeremiah is also weary of not being listened to. The verse reads, "But if I say, 'I will not mention him [the Lord] or speak any more in his name,' his word is in my heart like a fire, a fire shut up in my bones. I am weary of holding it in; indeed, I cannot."

The words burned in Robin's heart, too, and rekindled the fire of her calling, to reach those girls in the tent with the gospel. The girls' challenge to write books fit for them to read was her "Macedonia call," Robin says, referring to the vision Paul had of a man in Macedonia begging him to come to Macedonia and help him (Acts 16:9). Robin just needed to keep praying someone else—a publisher—would also catch the vision.

While at a writers conference in 1988, Robin learned that Focus on the Family was starting up a publishing program and might be looking for material for teens. She sent the manuscript to them. Five days after they received it, one of their editors called.

Robin vividly recalls that day. "It was Martin Luther King Day, and the kids were out of school. I was in the front yard, holding my baby daughter and watching my son on his tricycle. We lived on a busy street, and he couldn't be out by himself. When the portable phone rang, Rachel was crying, and my son was sailing out of sight down the street. When Janet from Focus told me that this is just what they'd been looking for, I thought it was a dream come true."

Focus on the Family was gearing up for the dedication of their new building in Pomona, California in two weeks. Robin realized she was heading down that way to visit her parents anyway. Janet invited her to lunch. Robin drove down with the kids, left them with her mother, and went to lunch with all the "big names" at Focus, who introduced her as "the new teen fiction author."

"I was floating," Robin says.

Robin returned to her mother's house—back to reality. When she picked up her crying baby, Rachel threw up on her new dress. "After my moment in the sun, the rest was just a lot of work," she says with a laugh.

Robin is not exaggerating about the work. Focus asked for more books, and Robin complied.

During the next decade, she wrote eleven more Christy novels and twelve Sierra Jensen novels. The pace picked up when she agreed to write the GLENBROOKE SERIES, and for six years in a row Robin wrote five books each year.

During that time, she put her husband through seminary. Her family moved eleven times; her husband changed jobs; they were on staff at five different churches, some of which endured church splits; and Robin went through three major surgeries.

What kept her going was always that original vision. "First it was my calling to reach those teenage girls in the tent, and then it became my passion." She came to think of these girls as her "unreached people group." She *was* a missionary of sorts, but one who used undercover methods for smuggling truth into young hearts. A quote by C. S. Lewis in a letter to his friend Arthur Greeves served as a focus for her writing: "Any amount of theology can now be smuggled into people's minds under cover of romance without their knowing it." Robin was giving these teens the romance she knew they would read, but at the same time she was smuggling theology into their hearts and minds. In fact, the twelve-book CHRISTY MILLER SERIES covered a twelve-step discipleship program that she and her husband used with kids—but it was clothed in fiction.

One of Emily Dickinson's poems says "Tell all the truth but tell it slant." Robin's "slant" is romance. The truth is that we are God's first love, and our hearts will not be settled until he becomes *our* first love. "This is the ultimate romance," Robin says. It's become her passion to introduce women of all ages to God as their relentless lover who will never give up until he woos them to himself.

Robin believes that each of us is uniquely gifted to convey some message about God. Writers do it in their stories. But all of us through our innate talents, personality, and experiences of God become uniquely gifted to communicate something of God's truth to the world around us. In fact, it becomes second nature to communicate it in all we do.

If you're not sure how God wants to communicate his truth through your life, Robin suggests taking time to look at yourself. Prayerfully ask God, "What have you uniquely gifted me to do?"

Look at those times when you really enjoyed something you did—no matter how small or insignificant the event may be. "You can tell when it's the Spirit and you're using your gift," Robin says. "The breath of God blows over you and you are energized." Look for the common thread in experiences in which you were so energized. That will point to your mission.

Once you know what that mission is, it serves as a focus for everything else. It's a grid through which you can run every opportunity, asking, "Is this in line with what I'm uniquely gifted to do?" If it's not, then you can say no and trust God has gifted someone else to do it.

As a teenager, Robin told God that she wanted to be a missionary, perhaps to Kenya. Years later, God has taken that desire and reshaped it to his own purposes. He showed her the "people group" he wanted her to reach, equipped her with the gifts to reach them through the most effective means (fiction), sustained her through the hard times, and blessed her beyond her wildest dreams.

Every so often she gets glimpses of what God is doing through her books. At an international writers conference she attended outside of London, she sat next to a woman from Kenya. The woman told her that she had read Robin's books in Kenya and now was a Christian and working for a publishing company.

God sent Robin to Kenya after all, but not as a laundry worker. He sent his message through her books, not her physical presence.

Another time Robin received a letter from a Jamaican woman who was serving time in prison in Panama for international drug dealing. This prisoner had read a copy of *Whispers* while she was in prison and come to Christ. She wrote Robin a poem about how her heart was free because she knew Jesus. "How that book ever got to a Panama prison, I have no idea," Robin says. "God has been in control from the beginning. What he is doing astounds me as it continues to unfold in amazing ways."

Robin has found that "when we take seriously those Macedonian calls that come to all of us, God uses them at every single point along the way. And all we can say is, 'Wow, I never expected it to happen this way.'"

God is ever a God of surprises, working in ways we would never imagine, so that the glory goes to him, not us.

CHAPTER 3

Everybody Needs Somebody

"Instead of a gem, or even a flower, if we could cast the gift

of a lovely thought into the heart of a friend, that would be

giving as the angels give."

— GEORGE MacDONALD

"Each friend represents a world in us, a world possibly not born

until they arrive, and it is only by this meeting

that a new world is born."

—ANAÏS NIN

JUDITH PELLA

"I am a storyteller. I have finally come to realize that stories can be savored just for the sake of the story. Pure escapism is a blessing to many, and I am happy to be used for this purpose."

JUDITH PELLA'S first published book was *The Heather Hills of Stonewycke,* the first volume in THE STONEWYCKE TRILOGY, coauthored with Michael Phillips. She went on to write fifteen books with Michael, eight of her own, and three with Tracie Peterson. Her most recent book is *Written on the Wind.* Judith lives in a coastal town in northern California with her husband and three children.

With a Little Help From a Friend

Though Judith Pella harbored a secret desire to see her name on the cover of a book, that's as far as she took her dream. Her call to become a writer never felt very definite; rather, it arose out of who God made her and an opportunity that came her way at the right time.

Judith can hardly remember a time when she wasn't making up stories in her head. She was a shy child who found it easy to lose herself in other worlds. Because socializing with others was so difficult, TV, movies, and reading became important social outlets for her. "In these worlds on screen or paper I didn't have to be a social misfit," she says. "I could become Rosalind Russell in the movie *His Girl Friday*—my ideal! I knew I could never be an aggressive, fast-talking reporter, but I could imagine myself as one and that was almost as good. Even better, I could write about one!"

That was the next logical step (although she says she didn't actually write her "Rosalind Russell" story until now, with *Written on the Wind*—her latest book). Other worlds and situations caught her fancy. At eleven, she was writing her version of *Rebel Without a Cause* and a Civil War spy story.

"Then I grew up," she says. "How sad that was!" Sad because she knew she had to plan her future, and that meant focusing on other things. Being a writer never entered the picture. Her family thought she was a bit odd, making up stories all the time, but it never occurred to anyone that this could and should be part of Judith's future.

Judith thought she should become a nurse. After all, she loved the Sue Barton books and the Dr. Kildare television series. "What a noble profession for a good Christian girl!" Judith says. "The only trouble was, I was a terrible nurse who was never sure of myself and quaked in the presence of . . . nearly everyone!"

Becoming a nurse and hating it was definitely a step away from her secret dream to see her name on a book. Another backward step, for a while at least, was when she renewed her Christian walk after she finished college. She explains, "Somewhere along the line I got the idea that telling stories, watching television and movies, and even reading fiction was something strong Christians just didn't do." Involvement with stories seemed frivolous in the circles in which she ran.

Slowly, however, she began reading fiction again—at first, fantasies like C. S. Lewis's THE CHRONICLES OF NARNIA and *The Lord of the Rings* by J. R. R. Tolkien. "I got to reading a lot, and nothing bad happened," Judith says with a laugh. In fact, something good happened—Judith was again in touch with an essential piece of herself, the piece that is nurtured by stories.

When going through a rocky time in her marriage in her thirties, Judith began writing stories again. It was more therapy and escape for her than any conscious career shift—"something enjoyable to do while my world was falling apart."

Michael Phillips, a friend of her husband, asked one day to see what she was writing. When Judith showed him, he said, "This is good!" Michael started talking about writing novels together.

"I didn't know if he really thought I had talent, or he was just trying to encourage me," Judith says. "I had never thought of the practical aspect of how to actually get published. But Michael knew." At the time Michael had edited several novels by the nineteenth-century novelist George MacDonald and was ready to write some of his own novels. He encouraged Judith to work with him, and together they brainstormed ideas for what would become the Stonewycke series, published by Bethany House.

Working with Michael on a book for publication was a walk of faith for a number of reasons. All along the way she battled the dragons of her own lack of confidence, her shyness, and the practical challenge of finding time to write while holding down her day job and taking care of her two children.

But the books sold, the publisher wanted more, and together Judith and Michael wrote six books in the Stonewycke series, three in a series set in Russia, and a couple of others. Eventually it was time to see if she could write books on her own, and she and Michael agreed to stay friends but not cowriters. Judith wrote ten solo books, including finishing the Russian series, along with several frontier books and a couple of contemporary books. Then she partnered with Tracie Peterson for six books in the RIBBONS OF STEEL and RIBBONS WEST series. She continues to write mostly historical novels, her first love.

Judith quit her job as a kindergarten teacher's aide shortly before finishing her first solo book, *Frontier Lady*, in 1991. Her reticent nature wouldn't have allowed her to take such a risk, but again it was an outside force that prompted this move. Her son needed some special attention, and she decided to be home full time with him. A few years ago, though, when she and her husband bought a new house, she wondered again if she should get another job that would bring in a steadier income than writing. Her husband said, "What for? Writing is what you're good at." And finally, Judith was able to embrace the truth: writing *is* what she's good at. Telling stories is what God has given her to do; this is what he's blessing.

Sometimes the gift a person has been given is so central to who he or she is—like Judy's storytelling—that it's difficult for that person to perceive the calling inherent in the gift. This is especially true if the gift is either not recognized as particularly valuable (as in Judith's case), or is taken for granted as a given (the whole family is good with their hands, say, so your dexterity seems like no big deal).

Don't let fear limit you from reaching toward your dream, Judith says. "As Christians, we limit God so much. In my own life, thinking I was serving him by becoming a nurse, I cut off that which he had planted in me from the beginning. I am so glad I finally woke up and rediscovered my storytelling roots."

Even if you don't heed the call until later in life, that's okay. As

Judith points out, "Even side journeys can be important instruments of growth. All the detours I've taken have only made my life that much richer with life experiences." In God's economy, nothing in your life needs to be wasted.

God can use anything to wake you up to the special talent that can lead to a calling, but often he uses other people. By God's grace, Judith got to know a writer who recognized her talent and was interested in encouraging her. Without Michael Phillips, Judith says she'd never have had the courage or knowledge to try to write for publication. If you are just beginning to tune in to your gift, pray that God might bring someone into your life who can offer encouragement, support, and practical knowledge. Seek out individuals who are doing what you long to do, and find out how they got there. God just may have a "Michael Phillips" waiting in the wings to launch you toward your calling!

MELODY CARLSON

MELODY CARLSON is the author of more than sixty books for children and adults. She won the RITA Award from Romance Writers of America in 1998 for her novel *Homeward,* and *Awakening Heart* was a finalist the following year. Her children's book *Benjamin's Box* was a finalist for the Gold Medallion and WOW Awards in 1998, and *King of the Stable* won the Gold Medallion in 1999. And a number of her children's titles have appeared on the ECPA (Evangelical Christian Publishers Association) bestsellers list over the past several years.

"I've reached the place in my writing where, more than anything, I want to honor God . . . to be sensitive to where he's leading me as a person and a writer. And it doesn't mean that every book I write will blatantly shout out the 'four spiritual laws' but rather (I hope) show traces of redemption, forgiveness, unconditional love, grace . . . and other positive aspects of real Christianity. I think that's what the 'gifting' of being a writer is all about."

Honor the Gift

It's not always easy to see our own gifts. Often the thing we do well, we do so naturally that we can't even see how we've been gifted until someone else (usually not so endowed) points it out to us.

That's the way it was with Melody Carlson and writing. She'd always loved to write, and her teachers told her she should consider becoming a writer, but somehow it never sank in. She did many other things after college and getting married: raised her two sons, taught preschool, started a child-care business in her home, and tried out a variety of other jobs that interested her.

But by her midthirties, something shifted for her. "I felt like I was choking," she says. "I wanted to write." For years she had been able to keep preschoolers enthralled with her stories for two hours at a time while the younger children napped. The stories were there. She itched to write them down.

She started writing longhand on a yellow pad. Then she switched to a typewriter. Then her husband bought her a computer.

A lot was happening at that time in her life—she looks back and marvels at the way God's hand was at work. She and her husband sold their home and built a new house. Melody stepped into an executive position with an international adoption agency. "It was fun, but I couldn't at the time understand why I was hired there," she says. "I didn't have any experience that would qualify me for that position." She held that position for a year, until an opportunity with a publishing company came up. "The doors opened, and our family felt God was calling us to move, so I took the position." Suddenly the purpose for that job with the adoption agency made sense: It was what qualified her for this new position. Being in publishing would give her wonderful hands-on experience with the whole business side of writing. She also thought it would give her more family time.

Meanwhile, Melody was also writing and sending out her work. In that first year she received many rejections, but she persevered. She joined a writers critique group. By that point she couldn't help but write. But she felt it was a selfish pursuit, something she did because it brought her joy. She did not yet see it as a gift or a calling. "I thought I would dabble until my sons were out of college," she says. "I had no idea that God was planning something else for my writing."

For three years Melody worked for that Christian publisher, while all the time pursuing her first love—writing fiction. Her writing sold. Eventually the publishing job started to take over her life, crowding out family time. Something had to give.

At a Christian Booksellers convention in the summer of '97, Melody had a conversation with Alice Gray that opened her eyes. Alice told Melody that she had a gift and she needed to be faithful to it. "It was the first time someone had ever said to me, 'You're gifted,'" Melody says. "Writing had always come so easily to me, I thought anyone could do it. Being in the publishing industry, I was around so many talented people, it was easy for me to feel like a nobody. But I respected Alice. I took to heart her sweet little lecture about honoring my gift. I think it was then that I realized writing was a calling."

Still, it took some time to adjust to this new way of thinking about herself. "It was hard to say 'I have a gift' because it was hard to see it." She needed a mirror. Alice Gray was her first mirror, opening her eyes to her gift. Her husband, Chris, also pointed out the same thing. A few months after her talk with Alice, she and Chris prayed about what to do about her job. Chris thought she should quit the job and write full time, even though they would be giving up financial security, since he was a contractor and they were heading into winter, the slow period in his business. He was willing to take that financial risk because he believed in her gift.

When Melody walked into her office the following Monday to tell them she was leaving, part of her felt perfect peace, and another part felt as if she were stepping into an abyss. "It was a faith walk all the way. My prayer was, 'Oh, God, this is your gift and your calling; what do you want me to do with it?' "

The time of testing came. Financially, it was tough for a few months. Though Chris's business immediately started to pick up— God's provision—Melody's writing income took a little more time. She enjoyed spending more time with her boys but had no big projects to work on. Then she went on a ten-city book tour—her "one and only book tour," she notes—when her book *My First Bible Brain Quest* came out with Workman Press. It was a wonderful time of connecting with people, and soon the ideas started flowing.

Then came the public confirmation of her gift and calling. Melody's books were nominated for several awards. When she won the prestigious Romance Writers of America RITA Award, she was dumbfounded. "Though I don't hold much stock in awards," she says, "coming when it did, at that low point, it was a real boost. I said to God, 'You have something going that's bigger than me— thanks.' " After that opportunities continued to build.

Now one of the biggest challenges for Melody is discerning whether or not God is behind an opportunity. Her career has to be in his hands, not her own. "I may say I won't do any more children's books for this year, and then a project comes along that looks like a wonderful opportunity, and I have to come before God again and ask, 'Is this from you or not?' "

She recalls a time she didn't do that. The project looked so easy, it seemed there was no need to even bother asking God about it. But the project turned out to be anything but simple. "Sometimes God does lead you to do something that's very difficult," she says, "but you can handle it because you know it's him. But that wasn't one of those times." If she had sought God, she probably would have felt that check in her spirit she has felt at other times, with other projects. She recalls turning down something that seemed like a good thing financially, but somehow she did not have the green light from God.

There is tremendous freedom in knowing that one's gift is from God. "It takes the pressure off," Melody says. "If one of my books doesn't sell well, then I can figure it's gotten to the people it's meant to reach." Leaving the results in God's hands allows her to focus on her task—to write the best books, with the truest message, that she can.

Melody Carlson might not have embraced her gift or discerned her calling without the encouragement and support of others. "The purposes of a man's heart are deep waters, but a man of under-standing draws them out," declares Proverbs 20:5. Gifts are best dis-covered by other people who point them out to us. If you don't know your gift, pray for God to send his wise ones who can draw them out for you.

And don't forget: You can be that person "of understanding" for others, as well.

JAMIE LANGSTON TURNER

JAMIE LANGSTON TURNER is the author of several novels, plays, poems, short stories, and articles. She is the author of *Suncatchers, Some Wildflower in My Heart, By the Light of a Thousand Stars,* and *A Garden to Keep.* She also teaches creative writing at Bob Jones University, where she and her husband have served for more than twenty-nine years. Her husband, Daniel, is chairman of the Music Education Department at Bob Jones, and they have one son, Jess, who is about to leave the nest.

"One thing I have taken on as a mission in my books is to smash a few stereotypes people have about fundamentalist Christians. I want to show there are many Christians who are totally sold out to the Lord, who also love art, can express themselves well, are intelligent and fair-minded, have a good sense of humor, and love life."

Influenced and Influencing

Jamie Langston Turner would not be a writer today if it weren't for her fifth grade teacher, Mrs. Hansborough. "She was *the* teacher in my life," Jamie says. "She began reading poetry to us after recess that year. I hadn't heard much poetry before this, so Mrs. Hansborough's reading had a tremendous impact on me. I had never heard anything so beautiful. It transported me."

That's when Jamie Langston started to write. She wrote poetry in her bedroom, by herself, and she also wrote a Nancy Drew type mystery story she called "Under the Waterfall."

One day she decided to show her teacher her work. "I remember the exact day," Jamie says, "and I have thought back on that moment many times. She read through my poems at a leisurely pace and made little murmurs of delight. 'Did you write all of this?' she asked at one point. And when she finished, she straightened the papers and asked me, 'Do you think I could have a copy of these?' I know now that if she had handled those poems less respectfully, I would never have written another one." Jamie labored to copy her poems for her teacher, and when she finally presented them, Mrs. Hansborough exclaimed, "Oh, my very own to keep forever."

"That's what it took to keep me writing," Jamie says.

It also inspired her to teach. "I loved my teacher so much that I also wanted to be a teacher to do for others what she did for me." In college Jamie majored in elementary education. She then taught fifth and sixth grades for ten years. During that time she also wrote. Every year she wrote a play for her students to perform. Some of these plays were even published. Once she won an extemporaneous essay contest.

"I kept feeling the pull to write," Jamie says. Eventually she went back to grad school and got her master's degree in teaching English.

When her husband began his doctoral work at the University of Illinois, Jamie started writing freelance and trying to get her work published. "I wasn't thinking of it as, 'I'm going to be a writer now,' but was just trying to find a way to make some extra money," Jamie explains.

She began to receive rejection slips. "I was mortified at first and threw them away as soon as I got them," she says. "Then I began saving them. I kept them in a box, and now I show them whenever I give a talk about writing. I tell my audience, 'This is a big part of my education as a writer.' "

Slowly some of her stories, plays, poems, and articles were accepted. After her husband finished his degree, they moved back to South Carolina, and she started teaching American literature, freshman English, and a writing class for education majors at Bob Jones University.

That's when she got a call from an editor at Moody Press, asking her if she would consider writing a novel for them. Her first response was, "I had thought of writing a children's book sometime." No, the editor said, they were looking for people to write *adult* novels.

"Well, I write short things," Jamie replied. But then she realized she had felt frustrated limiting herself to short pieces. "Think about an idea," the editor suggested.

Jamie did more than think. She wrote four chapters of a book called *Suncatchers* and sent it off. It took a long time for the editor to reply. He had moved to work for another publisher in the meantime, and Jamie eventually lost contact with him. A year later she finished the manuscript for *Suncatchers* and sent it unsolicited to Thomas Nelson Publishers. It was accepted, and in September 1995 *Suncatchers* was published.

In the meantime, she had found the idea for her next book—at her son's soccer game, of all places. "It was a six o'clock game," Jamie recalls, "on a dark and drizzly evening. There were only a few parents in the stands. I was behind a woman who was all hunched over and wrapped in blankets. I could tell by her body language that she didn't want to talk to anyone. But something within me said, 'Talk to her.' " At half time Jamie moved over to sit next to the woman and asked, "Do you have a son playing?" The woman, who Jamie could now see was much older, said, "Grandson." After a few more exchanges, Jamie asked if she went to church anywhere. "She looked at me with the most penetrating eyes and said, 'I have not been in a church since God allowed my daughter to be killed.' I thought, *That's my next book.* I wondered about this woman, what would make someone feel betrayed by God like that."

Jamie started writing *Some Wildflower in My Heart.* It was a difficult book to write, not only because it dealt with a difficult topic—sexual abuse—but because it required her to get under the skin of someone who was very different from her in many ways. "But I believe that God led me to that woman that night at the soccer game, and I believe he directed my thoughts when I sat down at the computer in the months to come."

But a publisher did not materialize. Her previous publisher turned it down, as did three others. Each said the book was too "literary" or "heavy." Her new agent urged her to think about rewriting it, making it "happier" and "an easier read." Jamie wasn't sure she should do that. It just didn't feel right to do so. Discouraged, Jamie felt very low for a couple of months. "I thought maybe I would be a one-book author," Jamie says, "and that this book would stay up in the attic in a box." But she began writing her third book anyway. "The ideas were still coming, I was still enjoying the writing, and I didn't feel the door was totally closed," she says.

She told herself that God could use this period of discouragement. Look at all the great art that artists have produced during low periods. She had read that John Steinbeck said of *The Grapes of Wrath,* "This is the worst book I've ever written, but I will finish it just to finish it." She figured God could use even her discouragement to make her a better writer: "It would help me write more effectively about discouragement in the lives of my characters."

Then she got a call from Bethany. They wanted to see the whole manuscript. A male editor had read the four sample chapters, and felt he should pass it on to a female editor before saying no. Bethany ended up buying the manuscript enthusiastically. "I got re-inspired again," Jamie says.

She's been writing—and continuing to teach—ever since. "I draw a lot of power from teaching, but it does take up a lot of time," Jamie says. "I teach creative writing, and it involves a lot of grading." Like most people, Jamie juggles many things—teaching, taking care of her family, church work, and writing novels. Some days she feels squeezed and wonders what needs to go. But one thing is certain: she'll keep writing.

"One thing I have taken on as a mission in my books is to smash a few stereotypes people have about fundamentalist Christians," she says. "In so many books Christians are portrayed as villains or buffoons, and this is the only picture some people have of us. I wanted to show there are many Christians who are totally sold out to the Lord, who also love art, can express themselves well, are intelligent and fair-minded, have a good sense of humor, and love life." She takes her craft very seriously and works hard to make each book something not only she, but also her Lord and fellow Christians can be proud of. "I feel very strongly that we as Christian writers have to reflect well on our Savior by the quality of the books we write," she says. "It's not enough to just write a good message. Horace said the best literature both delights and teaches. We want to write as beautifully as the secular writers, but we have truth as well."

This ethic of excellence applies to our lives, as well, Jamie would say. Her novels are often about the impact ordinary Christians can have on the people around them. Unbelievers are watching us. If they see people who are in love with God, with life, and with people, they will be drawn to the Source of that life view, and they will find healing. We may think we're just an ordinary person with nothing special to offer. But if we are connected to the Source of living water, we have something invaluable to offer the thirsty people around us. They are watching us, their thirst increasing the more they see Christ in us. Eventually they will ask us why we're not thirsty. And all we have to do then is point them to the Water of Life.

CHAPTER 4

Dream God's Dreams

"I believe our heart desires are the allurements of God, coaxing us

to a life beyond what we could ever ask or imagine. As we serve

God out of our desires, we find a fulfillment and satisfaction

like we've never known."

— DOUGLAS J. RUMFORD

KAREN KINGSBURY

"I try to use fiction to touch hearts and teach a truth. Christ used story to attract the crowds, to tend to the hardened soil that had gathered around the hearts of his people, and to prepare them for greater truth. This is what I attempt to do when I write a novel."

KAREN KINGSBURY is the bestselling author of fourteen books, including inspirational fiction titles *When Joy Came to Stay, A Moment of Weakness,* and *Waiting for Morning.* One of her earlier books, *Deadly Pretender,* was made into a CBS TV movie of the week. She lives in the Pacific Northwest with her husband and five children.

Reach for the Stars

Today Karen Kingsbury is known for writing emotionally gripping inspirational fiction—unforgettable tearjerkers. But that wasn't always the case. In fact, there was a time when Karen's work included reporting on sports events for a major Los Angeles newspaper. When she looks at where she's been and where she is today, Karen marvels. "I'm certain of one thing," Karen says. "My role as an inspirational fiction author was orchestrated completely by God alone."

Karen Kingsbury began writing at an early age—before kindergarten even—and by the time she was in high school she knew she wanted to be an author. She also knew the odds against that happening. So she followed her dad's advice: Dream big and have a backup plan.

The backup plan for Karen was journalism. There would always be jobs for reporters, she figured. She earned a journalism degree from Cal State University Northridge in 1986. In her senior year she worked as an intern for the *Los Angeles Times* sports department. After she graduated, she wrote sports and miscellaneous stories for a small newspaper, then she took a job in the sports department at the *Los Angeles Daily News.*

It was during that time that she met her husband, and the two began studying the Bible. By 1988, their searching resulted in two things: lives given over to the Lord and a commitment in holy matrimony.

Still young in her faith, Karen was rocked to learn six months later that she was pregnant. "I had always dreamed of being a mother," Karen says, "but the timing was all wrong." Her husband was a full-time student earning a teaching degree, and she had moved from the sports page to the front page in what was a very time-consuming and demanding job. "I was afraid my child would grow up in day care and I would miss out on the experience of a lifetime—raising children."

Karen's husband's answer was simple and filled with faith: pray. Pray every day, he told her, for God to provide a way for you to make a living writing at home. "I was skeptical at best," Karen admits. "How would I make my annual salary at home when I'd never so much as freelanced a single magazine article?" The mountain before her seemed daunting.

Still, she and her husband committed themselves to prayer. Halfway through her pregnancy, Karen sold a story to *People* magazine. The article appeared in September 1989, the same month that they welcomed their baby daughter, Kelsey. A few days later she received a call from a New York literary agent asking her about the story she'd written for *People*. That story, the agent told her, would make a great book. Was she willing to write it?

Karen was torn in a dozen directions. How could she hold a demanding full-time job, cope with the workload of being a first-time mother, and write a book at the same time? Not seeing the agent's request as an answer to prayer, Karen blindly wrote a proposal with a few sample chapters and a story outline. The agent loved what she'd written, and ten days before her maternity leave was up he called with good news. The proposal had gotten into a bidding war between two major New York publishing houses, and the advance would be three times her annual salary.

Karen dropped to her bed, her hand frozen to the phone. The agent continued, telling her that when she signed the contract she would get the first third of the advance and possibly no more for that calendar year. The math took only a few minutes. Karen realized that the first check would be $12.89 more than she made a year. It was a stunningly direct answer to the prayers she and her husband had uttered daily for her to have a way to be home with their newborn daughter.

That first book, *Missy's Murder*, was one of four true crime books Karen wrote with Dell Publishing. Another of the books, *Deadly Pretender*, was made into a CBS movie of the week. In the years that followed, she wrote four collections of inspirational stories under the pseudonym Kelsey Tyler. Although the books were written with a secular publishing house, they were Christian through and through. "I got a taste for what it felt like to combine my writing with making a powerful impact on people for Christ," Karen says.

About that time she began considering the greatest desire of her heart: writing fiction. Initially Karen thought God was calling her to write secular fiction with a moral message. But when she wrote her first novel, *Where Yesterday Lives*, she was told there was no place for it at her New York publishing houses. One editor told her that the book made her laugh and cry and that she couldn't put it down. But it wouldn't sell, the editor said, because it contained no sex or foul language. The editor added that she didn't think the book needed sex or bad language, but still there was no place in the market for it without that addition.

Refusing to cater to the whims of a worldly publishing community, Karen began searching her heart, asking God where he was leading. "I was discouraged but not dissuaded," Karen says. "I knew God had a plan for me to write fiction, so I continued to search for the place where he would have me be."

The answer came through a friend who recommended Karen take a look at inspirational or Christian fiction. At the time most of the fiction published in the Christian Booksellers Association (CBA) market was historical or prairie romance. Since Karen was drawn to neither of these genres, at first she did not think she could write for the CBA market. But after reading Randy Alcorn's book *Deadline*, she realized that the kind of fiction she wanted to write was, indeed, being produced in the Christian market. Since Multnomah published Randy Alcorn's books, Karen sent her first novel to the editors there and waited for a response.

Typically a response takes less than two months, but for Karen an entire year went by before Multnomah agreed to publish *Where*

Yesterday Lives. This waiting time was a difficult one for Karen. Finances were tight, and there were times when she wondered if perhaps God was calling her away from writing. "But every time I sought him, the answer seemed the same: Wait. The breakthrough will come at the appointed time." So Karen waited, and in the process allowed the Holy Spirit to work on her heart, guiding her to a place of appreciation for inspirational fiction. "By the time I signed my first Multnomah contract," she says, "I knew that writing fiction that teaches God's truth is far better than anything else I could have dared dream to do."

And today, with four bestselling inspirational fiction titles on the market, Karen knows that it wasn't only God's best for her. It was a dream come true.

Looking back in wonder, Karen says, "I learned a lot through my transition from reporter to author to inspirational fiction novelist. Mostly that when God has a plan, he'll see it through to fruition." In addition, Karen says it's important to dream big. "God knows the plans he has for us. And sometimes those plans are limited only by our own lack of faith."

Karen should know. She's had her sleepless nights agonizing over what God wanted her to do, nights when the way seemed anything but clear. But today, she can confidently tell people to reach for the stars, go for their dreams. And in the process, she says, allow God to use you and the gifts he's given you to achieve his wondrous purpose.

"I see myself as a smuggler of God's truth under the guise of fiction. I want readers to feel so caught up in the story that the truths sneak into their hearts . . . and then stay for a long, long time, providing light as they face their own challenges and struggles in love and life."

CATHERINE PALMER lives in Missouri with her husband and two sons. She has published more than twenty-five books and has won numerous awards for her writing, including a Christy Award for *A Touch of Betrayal.* Her books include *The Happy Room,* based on her childhood on the mission field, *A Dangerous Silence,* the A TOWN CALLED HOPE series, FINDERS KEEPERS series, and TREASURES OF THE HEART series, and the Victorian Christmas anthologies. She has also served as consulting editor for Tyndale House Publishers' HeartQuest line of romance novels.

Fairy Tales and Faith

Catherine Palmer's entrée into the status of "published author" was so dramatic and sudden, it was almost like a fairy tale come true. She would need that sense of "only God could do this" for the struggles that came once she was a professional writer.

Growing up as a missionary kid in Africa with only her sister as a playmate much of the time, Catherine always told stories and began writing them down when she was a teenager. But it wasn't until years later—after she'd married, gotten a master's degree in English, taught school, and had a child—that she began writing with the intent of publishing.

She had finished a long historical novel set in medieval times and sent it off to several publishers. They all turned it down. Her mother-in-law suggested she rewrite the story as a romance and enter it in a contest.

Why not? thought Catherine. She rewrote the novel and submitted it in a romance novel competition. To her shock, the manuscript won not only Best Historical Romance but Best of Show, as well. After accepting the award, she was swarmed by agents and editors eager to find out what else she'd written and to sign her on. "It was like Cinderella," she says. "I was even wearing borrowed clothes for the conference!"

As a Christian committed to her faith, Catherine asked the Lord why he had suddenly flung open this door so wide. "I knew he had placed me there and I knew he had a purpose, but I wasn't quite sure what it was. I knew as Christians we are to be lights, so I vowed to try to be a light." Through prayer and talking to other Christians, she began to understand that she could be a voice for God in the secular world of romance publishing.

From the start she decided several things. She would never compromise her Christian standards. Though she was writing romance, she made sure her hero and heroine were married before they expressed their love physically. "My editors would ask me why my characters were always in arranged marriages of one sort or another," she says. "I'd tell them I believe physical love belongs in marriage."

She wove faith into the stories she wrote. A quote from C. S. Lewis that Robin Jones Gunn shared struck her as much as it had Robin. Lewis said, "Any amount of theology can now be smuggled into people's minds under cover of romance without their knowing it." She began to see herself as a smuggler of God's truth into the minds of readers, using the tools of her trade: vivid characters facing real-life problems who find solutions through faith, love, and courage.

Letters from readers asking questions such as, "Are you a born-again Christian?" or saying, "My faith has grown through reading your stories" made Catherine feel the light of God was shining through her work.

Invitations to speak came her way, and Catherine accepted them all. No matter what topic she addressed, she always made it clear that she was a believer in Jesus Christ and that faith is important in her stories. After her talks, whether in question-and-answer sessions or privately, people often commented on her faith.

She let anyone she met know that she was a believer and that her faith was central to who she was, especially at writers conferences. In this way she found other believers who wrote romance novels. Her editors, "most of them Jewish women," she says, knew where she stood. So did her agent, who was involved in the New Age movement. When the agent faced a personal tragedy, Catherine was the first person she called, and she asked Catherine to pray for her.

In all these ways, Catherine felt the light was getting through to the darkness. But it was not easy. The publishing road was bumpy. The company that published her first book folded. After publishing a book with a second publisher, her editor left, and a new editor wanted her to rewrite a book she had already submitted. She moved to yet another publisher and sometimes didn't know what was happening with her books. Catherine learned that these were fairly typical problems any author encounters. With each setback, Catherine had to go back to God in prayer to be reminded anew that she was where God wanted her to be.

Her most difficult opposition, however, came not from those in the secular romance field, but from Christians. "A couple of times, someone would come up to me and say, 'I don't see how you can call yourself a Christian and write this kind of thing,' " Catherine says. "They would look at the book's cover—about which I had no say whatsoever—and judge what was inside based on the cover art. I would ask, 'Have you read the book?' They hadn't, but they judged the book—and me."

Criticism from other Christians stung. But her husband reminded her, "You have dedicated every one of those books to God." It was true. "My prayer over each and every book I write is that every thought and every word will be acceptable in God's sight, as it says in Psalm 19:14," Catherine says.

Though she felt she was where God wanted her to be, she constantly asked for direction and was open to change. Eventually she began to feel restricted. She longed to share more of the light, more explicitly. Her editors had no trouble with having her characters pray, but when she wanted to mention more about Jesus, they felt she was going too far.

Catherine struggled, wondering what to do. On the one hand, she had a worldwide audience. Whatever truth she could "smuggle in" was reaching many people. On the other hand, she was limited in the secular marketplace. One of the things Catherine came to believe very passionately is that when a man and a woman build their life together on the foundation of Christ, life will be so much richer. Yet she was unable to communicate that message in her writing.

At a Romance Writers of America convention in New York,

Catherine attended a seminar held by a fiction editor for a Christian publishing house. "It felt to me like stepping out of the world into a quiet, holy place," Catherine recalls. There she talked to Francine Rivers, who had been successful in the secular romance world but had moved to writing for the Christian market. Catherine asked Francine the question that burned in her heart: "How can you give up the opportunity of reaching so many people for Christ to write for a much smaller market?" Francine's answer changed her life.

"Francine said my books could strengthen women's faith *and* be used as a tool to share faith with unbelievers," Catherine says. "It wasn't an either/or choice as I'd been thinking." She realized that by writing fiction for Christians, she would not have to give up her goals of reaching women who did not yet believe. Instead, she could communicate that Christ was the foundation of any strong and healthy relationship.

Making the switch to Christian publishing, Catherine is now writing about characters who have faith but struggle when life throws them a curve ball. Her mission is to strengthen readers' faith in the Lord and to strengthen their marriages. "I like to think of myself as an encourager," she says. "I want to encourage people to make their marriages work, even through tough times."

In the letters from readers of her Christian books, Catherine saw Francine's words come to life. "My books are helping believers to grow, and people are giving my books to unbelievers," she says.

Her passion for shedding light and encouraging others, and her past experience in the secular romance field, soon opened another door. She was asked by Tyndale House Publishers to be a consulting editor for their new line of romance novels. "Suddenly I could see that those years in the secular market were training for what I was doing with the HeartQuest line," she says. "I felt like the vision for a uniquely Christian kind of romance was something God gave me years ago, and now Tyndale has embraced it."

It's not always clear why God has us in a certain place until his purposes are revealed at some later point. Not all of us are ushered into a career or ministry in sudden or dramatic ways, as Catherine was. There were many times she needed to look back on how she got to where she was and remind herself that she could not have opened those doors by herself. The key was her heart. She had committed her gifts to God from the outset and had vowed not to hide her faith but to let it shine forth boldly. Her purpose was to invest her talents so that people would know God's love for them and his standards for relationships. God directed that intent along a path she is still walking and still doesn't always understand.

At her church, Catherine went through a process of identifying her spiritual gift. It was mercy. She believes that her experiences of being judged by other Christians for writing secular romances strengthened her gift. She believes her gift is expressed not only through her writing, but in myriad other ways as she interacts with those people God brings into her life. "Mercy, forgiveness, reconciliation are themes that crop up again and again in my writing," she says. "I believe the spiritual gifts are expressed through whatever we do as believers. We can minister in any number of ways, as God leads and gives us opportunity. The important thing, to me, is that we do sense that God's purpose is being worked out through whatever it is we do. I am a writer whose job is to minister. The ministry aspect is crucial. Whatever I do, I will try to be a little light for him."

What kind of fairy tale might God write in your life if you give him your talent? How might he minister to others if you let your light shine brightly for him?

God asks, "Whom shall I send? And who will go for us?" Can you answer with Isaiah, "Here am I [Lord]. Send me!" (Isaiah 6:8)? Perhaps you have an ability to make people laugh or to encourage children. Perhaps you know best how to make meals, provide a listening ear, or clean houses. When your heart says, "Send me!" and your hands bear gifts, large or small, God will open doors!

JANE PEART is the author of several series of historical romance: WESTWARD DREAMS, BRIDES OF MONTCLAIR, THE AMERICAN QUILT, INTERNATIONAL ROMANCE, as well as THE ORPHAN TRAIN WEST trilogy and the EDGECLIFFE MANOR MYSTERIES series. She has also published more than 250 short stories. Jane grew up in North Carolina, was educated in New England, and now lives in California.

"God equips us for the role he expects us to play in his plan. Everything about us serves this purpose—i.e., our parents, home environment, childhood influences, our character, and personality. We all have certain talents that are God-given for the work we are to do."

Delight Yourself in the Lord

Jane Peart always wanted to be a writer. Growing up, she did the usual things budding writers do: read voraciously and worked on the school paper and yearbook. It seemed an impossible dream to become a writer, but she dreamed it nonetheless. She read books about it. She identified with Jo from *Little Women*, the girl whose heart's desire was to write. When Jane fell in love and Ray asked her to marry him, at first she said no, she wanted to be a writer.

"I'll support you so you can write," Ray promised. She married him, and he kept his promise. He bought her her first Selectric typewriter. His mother gave Jane a copy of *How to Write a Story and Sell It* by Adela Rogers St. Johns, and Jane studied it. She wrote stories, sent them out, and persevered.

She didn't tell many people what she was doing. "If you say you're a writer, people will inevitably ask where you're published," Jane says. "If you say you're not published, or that you're published in some obscure magazine they've never heard of, they look at you skeptically."

Finally Jane sold her first story. "They paid me ninety dollars for it; I was so thrilled," Jane says. "I still remember what I bought with that money: a pair of gray flannel slacks for my husband and a painting I liked but couldn't otherwise afford."

When she was pregnant with her first child, she went to hear author Ray Bradbury talk about writing. Something he said impressed her deeply. Bradbury said, "The only successful writers are people who are single or are divorced." In his view, a writer has to devote his whole life to writing; there is no room for family or a "normal" life.

His words strengthened Jane's resolve to prove him wrong. "I loved my husband and, after the children came along, being a mother," she said. Nevertheless, underneath, the doubt niggled at her. Was it really possible to have a normal life and be a writer?

Jane's writing helped to supplement her husband's income; he was working nights and going to school. Even with two small children, Jane kept writing. By this time a British women's magazine was buying just about every story she wrote. Jane wrote whenever she could, mostly during the children's nap times and at night after they were in bed and her husband was off at work.

Jane loved to write even though she felt a vague guilt about it; perhaps she was being self-indulgent, taking all this time to do what she loved to do. When requests came to teach Sunday school or do the thousand and one things mothers and church members are asked to do, she would often say yes. "But it was always a struggle, and it always took away time from what I longed to do—write," she says.

It was almost as if Jane had a secret life, since she didn't publicize the fact that she was a writer, feeling most people wouldn't understand. Instead, she tried to be "everything to everybody, and do the things that were expected," all the while trying to fit in the thing she most loved to do. It exhausted her. Social commitments and engagements were neither easy nor natural for her. Her thoughts often turned to Ray Bradbury's comment. Perhaps he was right. Yet this was the life she had chosen, to be a wife and mother, and with that came certain obligations.

The tension between "fitting in" and "being different" was not all in Jane's mind. In her culture at that time, in the '60s and '70s, writing was seen as a rather odd thing to do. One of her children came back from her first play date at a neighbor's house and said of the friend's mom, "She doesn't even have a typewriter!" Another time, when her daughter was about five, she asked Jane, "Why don't you do anything normal, like cake decorating or ceramics?" Such comments fueled Jane's sense that she was the proverbial square peg in a round hole. The more she tried to be "normal," the more uneasy she felt. She had no sense that her writing could be fulfilling

God's purpose for her—not until a Christian friend sent her a tract that changed everything for Jane.

The booklet was on Psalm 37, especially verse 4: "Delight yourself in the Lord, and he will give you the desires of your heart." Jane did love the Lord, but this idea that God *wanted* to give her the desires of her heart was revolutionary. What if God's purpose for her was to devote herself to writing, because that's how he made her? Just as her neighbor loved to decorate cakes, Jane loved to write stories. Why shouldn't writing be as valid in God's eyes, even if it wasn't in the eyes of her social circle? This Scripture made Jane think that maybe God did value what she was drawn to. "I began to realize that God wants us to be doing what he made us to do," she says. God made Jane to love being alone, to love thinking up characters and plot lines. She realized it was okay to quit comparing herself to other people and trying to be someone else's idea of a good wife and mother, and to start focusing on what God expected of her. She had all the necessary elements needed for the life of a writer: imagination, ability to be alone for long periods of time, dedication to goals, discipline to make time to work, willingness to simplify other areas of her life. All that was left was to commit her way to the Lord and to trust him (Psalm 37:5).

Jane started to let go of the guilt she had always felt when she'd say, "No, I can't do that" because she had to write. Instead, she sees guarding her writing time as part of the discipline of her calling. If God made her a quiet, imaginative person who would rather write than attend a party, then she should write and say no to the party without feeling guilty. Not that she doesn't stretch herself and do things she doesn't want to do that need to be done. But she no longer feels guilty about fitting writing into her life and making that a priority. Eventually, the little girl who wanted her mother to do "normal" things was able to see a woman who modeled how to balance family and career. (That daughter, by the way, is an artist. The other is a children's librarian.)

Jane is grateful for the way God allowed his Word to open her eyes to the truth about her gift, for it set her free. She is also grate-ful for the support of other people along the way. Her husband has always supported her writing both emotionally and tangibly, such as when he took care of the kids when she faced a deadline. Her mother-in-law gave her that useful book by Adela Rogers St. Johns that helped Jane to launch her career. Also, when she lived in the Bay Area of California, she was able to meet for a while with fellow writers who were serious about getting published. "Writers groups are ever so valuable," she says. Now that she has moved to northern California, she no longer has that kind of critique group, and she misses it. But she does correspond regularly with other writers she has met at writers conferences. "You can't do it alone," she says.

Another turning point for Jane came when she discovered Christian publishers. She had published five novels with a secular publisher, but that publisher was beginning to move toward more sexually explicit novels. "I had already made a conscious decision not to write that kind of book," Jane says. The idea for a historical series was taking root in her mind. At the same time, she learned that Zondervan was looking for historical fiction. She submitted a proposal for a family saga. Her BRIDES OF MONTCLAIR series be-came fifteen books in all. "I didn't have to put anything in I didn't want, or take anything out," she says. "It reassured me that I was on the right path, and fulfilling the purpose God had for me."

Jane Peart has come a long way since those early days when she felt guilty for doing the thing that gave her the most joy. Like many artists and others whose gift may take them off the beaten path, Jane has had to come to grips with being different. She has learned to embrace her differences rather than hide them or suppress them. She has sorted through desires that are truly selfish and therefore part of the sinful nature and those that come from the way God has made her.

The key for her, and for any one of us, is made clear in Psalm 37:4. "Delight yourself in the Lord." In the context of devotion to God, the deepest desires of the heart are pure and, according to Scripture's promises, will be satisfied.

ALTON GANSKY

ALTON GANSKY is the author of ten novels and counting. He brings an eclectic background to his suspense and mystery novels, having worked in such fields as accounting, advertising, and architecture. Today he is the senior pastor of High Desert Baptist Church in Phelan, California, where he resides with his wife and family.

"In my books, I try to get people to think, to examine something in their own lives. Though entertainment and story are important to me, my purpose is to challenge my readers."

Despite the Obstacles

Alton Gansky can't tell you how he came upon his urge to write stories. It certainly didn't come from his background. His parents were not very educated and seldom read anything. Nor were they churchgoing people who instilled in him a vision of spiritual things. They had Alton late in life, and his siblings were already grown when he came along. He was essentially an only child left to entertain himself. A voracious reader with a very active imagination, he could entertain himself for hours with stories he made up. Somewhere along the line he realized he could even write down those stories. A bubble of a dream to see his name on the cover of his own book emerged and would not quite float away or pop.

The dream of writing, unencouraged and hardly even defined in Alton's own mind, was soon submerged in other matters of life. He became a fire fighter and then worked as an architect for ten years. Then he went into the ministry, answering a call he'd felt but resisted since committing his life to Christ in high school. He became a pastor.

But there was another call on his life, similar to his calling as a pastor, yet distinctive. He had never lost his inner desire to write stories. "During all that time of doing other things," he says, "there was a nagging desire to write. I wrote a screenplay in college, I wrote book reviews and a few articles, but it was the thought of writing a book that most intrigued me."

However, that tiny flame needed fanning, and there was little in Alton's life to fan the flame. Oh, he communicated through his work as a senior pastor. And he feels that communicating is his primary gift as a pastor, as opposed to more administrative or counseling duties. But he still harbored a secret longing to see his own name on the cover of a book.

Not surprisingly, the wind that finally blew life into his flame came in the form of another person. God often uses other people in our lives to effect his plan, Alton notes. While serving as pastor in a San Diego church, he met a fellow minister who had the same compelling desire to write. Like Alton, this man had written several small nonfiction pieces, but set his sights on the novel. Alton Gansky and Jack Cavanaugh became fast friends, and Jack has remained a friend and mentor to this day.

Alton eventually left San Diego to accept a position in Ojai, California, about two hours north of San Diego. While there he wrote his first novel, *By My Hands*. "Still among the uninitiated, I sent the book off to an 'agent,' one of those agencies you pay to look at your work," he remembers ruefully. "I have since learned that many agents who charge a reading fee are less than reputable." The "agent" had someone read it who sent it back with some notes, saying he couldn't use Alton's work. "None of the comments were very severe and the problems could have been easily fixed," Alton says. "But I didn't know that at the time."

He set the manuscript on a shelf and left it there for five years. "The urge to write was relentless, but I pushed it to the back of my mind," Alton says. There it stayed until one day Jack Cavanaugh called to share his good news. He had just signed not a one-book deal but a contract for a series!

"I rejoiced with him," Alton recalls. "Then he asked the question, 'So, what are you working on these days?' I thought of every excuse I could offer, but finally just said, 'Nothing.' There was a long pause, then Jack asked the question that changed my life: 'Why not?' "

Alton had no answer. He could plead the difficulties of his work, the challenges of ministry and family life, but he knew the excuses would fall on unsympathetic ears. Jack was a pastor and a family man, and had succeeded in answering his call. Why couldn't Alton?

Alton picked up *By My Hands* again and reworked it, then sent it off to Victor Books. They bought it. Alton has been writing books ever since—and loving it.

"Something was missing in my life when I wasn't writing," Alton says. "I didn't feel that sense of fulfillment. When I again started writing, I felt complete. I get depressed when I don't write. Despite the difficulties—and there are many challenges to writing—I feel I am doing something I was meant to do."

When a person begins to open up to latent gifts and desires, obstacles immediately present themselves. For Alton Gansky, the obstacles to writing have always been many. The first is simple inertia—getting started. "I liken it to hard exercise," he says. "It works, it makes a difference, and we're better for having done it, but oh, those lonely hours of concentration, analysis, and creative application! Creative ideas come in a moment; creative production comes after long, sweaty hours plowing the rocky fields of the mind." Substitute your own endeavor here. It's all hard work! Only the sense of purpose, of being called, and the fulfillment from using your gifts provide the energy to persevere.

Another obstacle for Alton is the industry itself. It is difficult to break in. This is true of other endeavors, as well. No matter what you want to do, you need some kind of preparation, and then you need to knock on doors. As Alton has found, "prayerful persistence is the only way in." But if God is the One calling you to the work, he will open the doors, in his own way and in his own time. Your job is to keep doing what you're supposed to do.

Other obstacles are more internal. Alton admits to "a regular cycle of fear." First there was the fear that he would never publish a book. After he did publish, he feared being a "one book wonder." Most writers, he has found, exchange one fear for another. Paradoxically, though, Alton embraces the fear. "It keeps me humble and in touch with God, the source of my calling. It reminds me I have been given a gift that can also be taken away, and that I serve at the pleasure of another."

Another potential obstacle may be circumstances that seem to prevent fulfillment of the call. One may ask, "How can a senior pastor find the time to write two novels a year?" The answer is both theoretical and practical. Alton's calling is to write. He points out,

"Even if my books sell a modest five thousand copies, that's five thousand people my words have reached. That's like pastoring a megachurch." The potential ministry justifies the time spent.

On the practical side, he believes that a pastor's role is not to run the church himself, but to equip the people in the church to do the work of the ministry (Ephesians 4:12). To that end, Alton has worked to make sure his church functions well without him. He focuses on his main gifts and calling—teaching and writing—and the church does the rest. He purposely takes his month of vacation time in one lump sum, to give the church practice in functioning without him. Once he understood his calling clearly, he focused on how to make it work in the light of his other responsibilities.

Alton believes that when a deep desire continues to nag at a person's heart, it's time to listen up. He advises taking the decision to the Lord in prayer and asking God to clarify the gift and how it is to be used to bring him glory in the world. When the voices of fear and other objections clamor, lay those obstacles before the throne of the Almighty. If a desire is of God, two things will happen: new opportunities will open up, and there will be an inner experience of peace. That inner peace is essential, Alton says. "I have learned, through some hard experiences, that if I don't have the peace of God about a decision, then I should not walk that path; it is the Holy Spirit's way of telling me I'm on the wrong course. And if I *do* possess a sense of peace, it is God's grace-filled blessing and I should walk that road."

Perhaps this is the hallmark of a calling: this sense that you are meant to do something, the restlessness that comes when you don't do it, the deep satisfaction you feel when you do it—whatever "it" is.

How do you find "it"? Ask yourself, "What is it I have loved doing, what has given me that sense of satisfaction? What would I do if I had two days to do whatever I wanted? What do I tend to gravitate toward and make time for? What do I feel passionate about? What have I always dreamed of doing?" These questions may begin to uncover that thing you do, or would like to do, that is your gift and perhaps your calling.

LAWANA BLACKWELL is a protégée of Gilbert Morris, who encouraged her to keep at her writing and never give up. She heeded his advice, and published three popular series: the VICTORIAN SERENADE series, the GRESHAM CHRONICLES series, and the TALES OF LONDON series. Lawana lives with her husband and three sons in Baton Rouge, Louisiana.

"My first calling is to be the best wife and mother I can be. My second calling is to write Christian fiction—that is, novels that show the gospel message and its impact on the lives of my characters."

Never Too Late

As Lawana Blackwell approached her fortieth birthday, she felt a restlessness. Something was missing in her life, but she wasn't sure what. Her life was full: husband, three children, ministries at the church, and a deep faith that tied everything together.

Still, she was restless. Something was stirring in her, a dream sparked long ago. And when she saw an ad for a novel-writing class at the local university in Baton Rouge, she knew what it was. She wanted to write fiction.

As a child, Lawana and her friends used to put on plays at school during recess. Making up stories was pure joy. She never dreamed, at that time, of becoming a writer—writers were such exalted creatures, in her mind. At age twenty-three, she wondered if possibly she could be a writer. The dream ignited and she wrote a story. "It was so bad, I threw it away and told myself becoming a writer was a pipe dream," Lawana says. The only time she indulged in writing was to create skits for the annual church retreat. People told her she had a gift for stories, but that encouragement barely fanned the dying embers of her dream.

But at age forty, Lawana realized the dream had not died. She may have doused the fire with her own doubts, but still the coals smoldered. "I was allowing fear of failure to keep me from trying," she says. "I was like a person who will not enter a race because she's afraid of failing. But the person who finishes last in the race is still further along than someone sitting on the sidelines, like me. I realized I was already failing by allowing fear to paralyze me. Would I look back in another forty years and regret what might have been?"

She looked again at the ad for the novel-writing course. For the past five years, she'd seen that ad and found reasons why she couldn't do it. Not this time. She signed up and was thrilled when the teacher, a published author by the name of Martha Corson, said she would critique up to fifteen pages a week. "I felt she was offering me gold," Lawana says. "I needed a published writer to tell me if I could do this. I had no idea if I had a gift."

Every week Lawana worked hard and turned in her pages. Ms. Corson wrote encouraging things on her work, but Lawana figured she did that for everyone. On the day of the last class, the teacher stood up and told the class that they all had talent, and there were three people she was advising to join the Romance Writers of America organization because they were already ready to pursue publishing. Lawana felt crushed, assuming that the three people already knew who they were. But when she got her final manuscript pages back, she read the words, "Your writing is of professional quality. I suggest you join RWA." Someone she trusted was telling her she could do this, she had the gift!

Lawana went down with Ms. Corson and the two other students to New Orleans for an RWA gathering. Though she was introduced to successful writers and her instructor offered to recommend Lawana to her editor at a major New York publisher, Lawana felt a strange discontent nag her. Somehow she didn't belong there.

"I didn't know then that there was a Christian presence in the RWA," Lawana says. Though the doors to publishing fiction seemed to be opening, Lawana felt unease rather than joy.

Shortly after that, she went on a church retreat. "I was sitting in the auditorium, and God spoke to my heart distinctly: 'Why don't you write Christian fiction?' " Though Lawana knew very little about Christian fiction, the desire to write burst into flames, fueled by the thought that she could write from her Christian convictions.

Now she had to find out how to get published in the Christian arena. She did a little homework and discovered that Christian author Gilbert Morris lived right there in Baton Rouge, and his number was in the phone book! It took three days of prayer for Lawana to muster the courage to call him. He said he was busy and would call back. More waiting—two months of waiting before Gilbert

Morris finally returned her call. But it was a call worth waiting for, because Dr. Morris was forming a writers critique group and invited her to participate.

"He made us work hard," Lawana reports. Gilbert Morris believed that if you say you want to write, you write; you don't just play at it. Lawana stayed up sometimes until three in the morning to write. She was homeschooling her youngest son at the time, and she had to fit writing into an already full life. "I had to learn how to make time for the things that were important to me," she says. "Writing had become very important to me."

Lawana told no one but her family what she was doing—lest she fail and become a laughingstock. But instead of failing, she landed her first contract. Then a second, and a third, until Lawana Blackwell realized she truly was a writer. What had been a pipe dream at twenty-three and a possibility at forty became a reality by age forty-three.

Looking back, she realizes that part of the reason she waited so long was that she wanted God to map out every step of the way ahead of time. She wanted to know if she would succeed before she even tried. But God didn't work that way. "He kept the door closed until I stepped out in faith," she says. She had to step out—not knowing if she had talent, not knowing if Gilbert Morris would be interested in helping her, not knowing if a publisher would offer her a contract. Then the doors opened, one by one.

Now Lawana Blackwell knows her calling, her ministry: to present the gospel and Christian truth through good fiction techniques. "Through fiction, I can reach people who would never pick up a devotional or other Christian nonfiction book," she says. "But they will read a good story. I always make sure the gospel is in the first book of each of my series, in some form. Other books explore how a Christian lives out his or her faith, how faith makes a difference in how they approach problems. People identify with the characters and receive biblical truth even if they don't realize it. Fiction can go many places where nonfiction can't."

Lawana Blackwell is living proof that it's never too late to rekindle a dream. The restlessness she felt upon turning forty was a good thing; perhaps it was the Holy Spirit stirring up the gift she didn't even know she had.

Is there a dream you've put on the back burner of your life? Have you been telling yourself it's too late to fulfill it? Lawana says don't give up yet. She points to her mentor, Gilbert Morris, who didn't begin writing until he was in his midfifties. "If you believe it's too late to use whatever talent God has given you, please reconsider," she says. "Get that dream off the back burner and start cooking!"

God just may have a whole feast in mind with your creation as the entrée.

CHAPTER 5

Not By My Strength

" 'Not by might nor by power, but by my Spirit,'

says the Lord Almighty."

— ZECHARIAH 4:6

"I myself do nothing. The Holy Spirit accomplishes all through me."

—WILLIAM BLAKE

"Our God specializes in working through normal people who believe in

a supernormal God who will do His work through them."

—BRUCE WILKINSON

JANETTE OKE

"My calling has been to present biblical truth through my books—my paper missionaries—and to respond to the letters I receive. I think my books have touched people because I write about love. People are so hungry for love."

JANETTE OKE is a pioneer in the world of Christian fiction. Her books were published at a time when little fiction was being published by Christian authors. Her first book, *Love Comes Softly,* zoomed to the bestseller list within six months, and the eight-volume series by the same name is still selling steadily more than twenty years later. In part because of the success of her fiction, Bethany House Publishers and other Christian publishers began to take a chance on publishing more and more fiction. Since her first title, Janette has published more than thirty-nine adult fiction titles and eighteen children's books. She has also coauthored several books with T. Davis Bunn. Janette Oke's books have made a great impact on publishing as well as on countless individuals' lives.

Keys to Ministry

As far back as she can remember, Janette Oke was interested in writing. She was a writer for many years before she was ever published, writing mostly for simple self-expression. "I was writing just for me, as a way to sort things out," she says.

She longed to receive special training in writing. "But it never happened," she says. "My husband, Edward, and I were in ministry. We had four kids. There was neither time nor money for training to be a writer."

But when the children were in their teens, Janette felt God nudging her. She had this book idea . . . and still no training. She prayed a lot about the whole matter. "I told God I would write this book, and if I had any talent I would give it all to him," Janette says. "Then God showed me that I had it backwards. He wanted everything right then. So I released my writing and that particular work to the Lord."

Reflecting back now, Janette is glad she never received any training. "I might have gotten the idea that I am smart enough to write books on my own. The way it was, I had to rely totally on God's help." Each book is bathed in prayer from beginning to end. "I want to make sure I write the words God wants me to write."

She has found great peace in releasing her writing to God. "I don't have to carry the burden of worrying about sales or bestseller lists or any of that. I told him everything was his. Whether something wonderful happened or nothing at all, it was up to him."

What to write was not difficult for Janette. "I was a fiction reader, and at that time there wasn't much fiction being done in the Christian community. I felt as Christians we were responsible to provide our readership with alternative fiction. I couldn't find much on the shelves that was compatible with my Christian perspective on life."

So Janette wrote the book she wanted to read.

Now it was time to find a publisher. She sent it to a secular publisher; it was rejected. She did her homework and realized she was supposed to use a different approach and send a query first. "I prayed a lot about a publisher," she says. One day, she drew a card from her little "promise box," a small box with cards containing a thought for the day on one side and a Scripture verse on the other side. She sometimes turned to this when she needed encouragement or direction. On the opposite side from the Scripture verse was a four-line verse, and midsentence was the word *Fellowship*. She thought it odd that it was capitalized like that. She went to the library and looked up whether any publishers had the word *Fellowship* as part of their name. Sure enough, one did. Bethany House Publishers was at that time publishing as Bethany Fellowship. Not knowing whether it meant anything, Janette sent her query to Bethany Fellowship.

Carol Johnson from Bethany wrote a postcard saying she would like to see the manuscript. "I almost wept when I saw it was signed by a woman," Janette says. "I thought if anyone would understand what I was trying to do, it would be a woman. There are so many people out there who don't read nonfiction, and no one was meeting their needs. I wanted to minister to those people who loved to read fiction."

At the time, Bethany was taking a huge risk, because no one knew whether those readers were really out there. Janette believed they were, but there was little proof that Christians had any appetite for fiction.

Love Comes Softly was published in July, and by Christmas it was on the bestseller list. Bethany approached Janette for a sequel. "I was scared," Janette confesses. "I had not even considered a sequel." Fear brought her to her knees again. "I did not want to let myself believe that the first book succeeded because of me. I never want to lose that sense of total dependency on God, or to start to think I can write a book on my own."

Another matter for prayer came as a result of a reader's letter. A woman wrote that her husband was not like the hero in Janette's romance—and she wished he were. This troubled Janette deeply. "I wanted to help marriages, not hurt them," she says. "I would not write if I thought I would be weakening a real marriage. I really struggled with this for a while." Through prayer, she came to the conclusion that even Jesus was misunderstood at times. "Being misunderstood doesn't mean you give up," she realized. "It does mean you are very careful to seek God's direction."

Janette answers every reader letter in some way, and she sees this as just as much a part of her calling as the writing itself. She welcomes the views of those who differ from her. "The readers who have challenged me have been a blessing to me. I've gone back to Scripture to find out why I believe as I do. These readers have helped me grow in my Christian life."

After reading her book *The Calling of Emily Evans,* a historical novel about young women who went out to start missions, some readers wrote to Janette questioning whether women can be called to the ministry. "I went to the Scripture and shared with my readers what I had learned," Janette says. She also reminded them that she was writing history, and there really were a number of young women who went out and started churches. In fact, that happened in her own town of Headley. "I don't know where I would be spiritually if Miss Pearl Reist had not come to our town and started a church. That fact of history was instrumental in changing my life."

Through readers' letters, Janette has learned how powerful the written word is. "Readers write and say my books have changed their lives. I think fiction can be powerful because there are no walls. Readers do not feel confronted. They can accept a message in the context of a story that they would never accept if someone just spoke to them." She adds that many readers would never pick up a Christian nonfiction book, but they will pick up a novel. Through her writing, she is able to present biblical truths in stories that can reach straight to the heart.

Janette Oke does not kid herself about her own part in this. She attributes any life change on the part of her readers to the Holy Spirit, not her own talent. "All of us have been given talents," she says. "But a *gift* is a talent that is used for ministry. Any ministry that is accomplished is done through the Holy Spirit." She stresses that writing fiction is only one way to minister. "We as Christians must be willing to use any means." Any talent you have may be the vehicle of God's special work of bringing blessing to others.

The question is, have you surrendered it? You may think it's only a little talent. Janette suspected she had some writing talent, but never had any formal training. Her great secret has been her knowledge of her personal limitations and her utter dependence on and surrender to the God who has no limitations. You have access to the same secret. The keys to Janette's sense of fulfilling her call are surrender and humility. These same keys unlock the door to your destiny, as well.

"Edifying the Bride of Christ is my goal. I want to make learning 'truth' enjoyable. I want the reader to be able to take something away that's lasting, not just tickle their ears."

LINDA CHAIKIN is an award-winning writer of more than eighteen books. She has written *Silk, Under Eastern Stars,* and *Kingscote,* set in missionary William Carey's India, along with EMPIRE BUILDERS, THE WINDS OF ALLEGIANCE, and the DAY TO REMEMBER series. *For Whom the Stars Shine* was a finalist for the Christy Award in the year 2000. Linda and her husband make their home in San Jose, California.

Yielding

L inda Lee Chaikin was born the youngest of ten children in a very poor family in rural California during World War II. Her father died when she was five months old, leaving her mother with eight young children and two brothers over age eighteen to raise on very little money.

Linda suffered with asthma throughout her childhood and spent most of her grade school years alone. Although they lacked material things, Linda's mother provided her with plenty of love and books to read. No matter how skimpy the budget, her mother somehow always managed to scrape together enough change to buy Linda the Little Golden Books that she loved so much. "She would usually buy them at the drugstore on the way home from seeing the doctor," Linda recalls. "I'd lie in bed and read and reread those little books, and my imagination would come alive." She also recalls the thrill of receiving a large book of Grimms' fairy tales one Christmas. "These books became the friends I didn't have the opportunity to make in school," Linda says. Though she was behind in subjects like math, she excelled in reading and spelling. Her proudest moment was when the teacher moved her up to the highest reading circle in her class.

"Out of these experiences," Linda says, "I have seen the promise of Romans 8:28 fulfilled in my life. God has worked all these things together for good. I'm certain God used some of my limitations to prepare me to become a storyteller."

During her teenage years, Linda began rewriting endings to the novels she was reading because she was dissatisfied with the original endings. Teachers often read aloud to the class the essays and short stories she wrote for school assignments. This confirmed her desire to become a novelist. At age fourteen, she wrote her first full-length novel, using a pen and a pad of paper. "I was actually like Jo in *Little Women*," she says, "who always had ink stains on her fingers!" Later, one of her seven brothers got her a typewriter. In those days, Linda could write anywhere, even in a room full of people and the television blaring.

She sent her novel off to a New York publishing house, convinced it would be another *Gone With the Wind*. What a heartbreak to receive the manuscript back with a rejection slip. (That novel, rewritten years later, was released under the title *Wednesday's Child* in the DAY TO REMEMBER series.)

Still, Linda Lee's driving ambition was to become a published author. She began writing a romance novel that contained things in it that she says "would corrupt the minds of the readers." One day at noon, when Linda was in the middle of writing her romance, Linda's mother turned on the radio, and the late J. V. McGee's voice came across loud and clear. "What's keeping you from yielding your entire life to the Lord, my friend? What's your little ewe lamb—the thing that is keeping you from God? Is there anything in your life that means more to you than knowing Jesus Christ and obeying his will?"

Linda knew the Lord was speaking directly to her through those words. "I knew exactly what that 'idol' was," Linda says. "That ambition that I would not surrender to his lordship because I felt that if I couldn't write, I couldn't be happy." After the radio program, Linda paced the living room floor for half the afternoon with that half-finished manuscript in her arms. "One would have thought it was a solid bar of gold," she says. "In reality, it was nothing except hay, wood, and stubble."

At the time, Christian publishers were not publishing fiction. Most publishers did not accept stories with an overt Christian theme. The choice then was "you either wrote to feed the unbeliever's old nature, or you just didn't write," Linda says. "I knew I was being asked to make a clean break, whatever the cost, even if it meant I would never write and sell my work."

Finally Linda walked over to the trash can and dumped the whole manuscript in it. "I knew if I kept it in the closet I'd be tempted to go back to it once something went wrong in my life that discouraged me," she says. Linda did not write again for many years.

She spent several years in intense Bible study. She got married. She taught Bible classes for teens and children in her neighborhood, which she counts as a special privilege. She was content in God's will. "I forgot all about writing novels and didn't miss it at all," she says. "I learned that the Lord alone satisfies and that I need not fear surrendering my will to him."

One day Linda's husband, Steve, bought her some books by C. S. Lewis. "I was deeply impressed with the clear demonstration of good and evil in his novels," she says. "It was as though the Lord was showing me that there were ways to write fiction that would honor him."

Linda had great fun writing a huge fantasy trilogy of her own. When Steve started reading it, he became so interested in the characters that he forgot it was his wife who wrote it. Impressed with his wife's talent, he bought her a computer and encouraged her to write. So Linda began writing historical fiction and romantic suspense, dealing with the struggles and temptations of Christians living in dark times. After receiving several rejections from various publishers, her first book was finally accepted and published in 1990. "I was thrilled that the Lord gave my writing back to me," Linda says. She's written eighteen books since then, most of which are still in print, "so I've made up for lost time!"

Linda Lee Chaikin believes now that God has called her to write, and she prayerfully considers what he wants her to say in each book. She carefully researches the historical background and includes solid biblical truth. "I want the reader to be able to take something away that's lasting, not just tickle their ears," she adds.

She loves what she is doing. "My life verse is Jeremiah 29:11," Linda says. "God knows his plans for each of us, and that should cause each of us to rest our head on our pillow each night with peace and contentment no matter what our calling in life."

Another verse that means a lot to Linda is Philippians 1:6, which says, "Being confident of this, that he who began a good work in you will carry it on to completion until the day of Christ Jesus." God began a work of making Linda into a writer, but when her heart turned from him, he took it back. Eventually, when she was ready, he gave back her love of writing and blessed it for his purposes. But as Linda reminds us, "This wonderful promise is for all God's children." Whatever God begins, he will finish—in his own time and his own great way.

LORI COPELAND was a bestselling romance author before she made the switch to writing for Christian publishers. She is the author of the BRIDES OF THE WEST series, several novellas, and the women's fiction title *Child of Grace,* as well as coauthor with Angela Hunt of the HEAVENLY DAZE series. She and her husband, Lance, have three grown sons and five grandchildren.

"When I start a book, I pray for guidance, wisdom, and to be used, whatever comes out on the page. I then move forth, confident (well, most times) that the book will do what the Lord wants it to do. And don't ever believe Christians aren't funny people. We have the most to smile about."

A Willing Heart

Lori Copeland grew up in the church and can't remember a time when she didn't believe in God. "Not that I always *gave* him my best, especially in the teenage years," Lori says. "But I always had a willing heart toward him."

Lori considers herself about as ordinary and unspectacular as a person can get. "I consider myself the vanilla pudding of the world." She got married at age seventeen to Lance before she finished high school. She had to go back and get her GED. She's attended a few college English courses but mainly threw herself into raising three sons. When her oldest son left the nest and her other two boys were teenagers, Lori had a little more time on her hands. She worked part time at a bank and read a lot.

Ideas for stories of her own started forming in her mind. A few people asked her, "Why don't you try to write a romance? With your zany outlook on life, I bet you could write a funny romance!" *No way could I write a book,* Lori thought. But one day, just for fun, she sat down and began writing a story.

When she finished, she didn't know what to do with it. She checked one of the books she was reading and sent the manuscript off to Silhouette at the address printed in the front of the book. "I didn't send a query letter, didn't know a thing about how to do this professionally," Lori says. "I had no idea how many words I needed for a Silhouette romance novel."

In a few weeks, the manuscript was returned with a standard rejection letter. Lori next sent it off to Dell, thinking, *What do I have to lose?* Four weeks to the day later, she got a call from Dell.

Thinking it was a magazine phone solicitor, Lori said, "I don't want any."

"Oh, I think you do," said the voice on the other end of the line, who turned out to be Lydia Paglio, an editor at Dell, who wanted to buy her manuscript! ("I had to stuff a Kleenex in my mouth to keep from laughing," Lydia said.) Lydia told her the manuscript was too short; the story would have to be beefed up and needed to include three love scenes. "They don't have to be graphic," the editor said, "but they have to be in there."

"That put the skids on for me," Lori says. She discussed it with Lance. "I don't think this would be right for us," Lori said. Lance said, "Well, why don't you just try one and see what happens."

Lori struggled over it. "What I wrote then is too graphic now for me," she says. But it was acceptable to the publisher. After reworking the manuscript, Lori received a three-book contract. For the next fifteen years, her books kept selling and she kept getting offers for contracts.

Though she was making a lot of money and gaining recognition, it didn't make Lori happy. "I was miserable the whole time," she says. "There was something inside me saying this is not what the Lord wants for you. You are his child. Act like it. *I have given you a talent to serve me,* the still, small voice said. *But I have also given you free will.*

"Today I would say publicly that the graphic sex scenes in romance novels do not glorify God nor build his kingdom. I would give the world if my old books were not still available, but sometimes we live with our mistakes."

Lori searched for alternatives. She learned of a Christian literary agent and called him. "I think the Lord wants me to switch and write fiction for the Christian market," she told him.

He discouraged her. "The Christian market isn't interested in your brand of humorous fiction," he told her. "Christians aren't very funny people." *Oh my. How sad,* Lori thought.

She kept praying for an open door somewhere. Or should she stop writing altogether? That didn't seem right; letters kept arriving from readers praising the small but nevertheless present message in Lori's secular work. The door had opened so suddenly and so completely, and the Lord had blessed so mightily. So Lori kept praying for a way out.

One day she was in Jefferson City, Missouri, for a book signing. She remembers lying on her hotel bed, looking up at the ceiling, telling God, "If you'll open the door, I'll walk through it." She thought of calling Catherine Palmer, who lived in Jefferson City. She and Catherine had met, and each knew the other was a Christian.

Catherine was glad to hear from Lori and said that she had been thinking of Lori because she had just become a consulting and acquiring editor for Tyndale's new romance fiction line. Before Lori left town that evening, Catherine had called Tyndale and was authorized to offer Lori a contract for a three-book series for their new HeartQuest line.

Suddenly the doors that had been shut for so long swung wide open.

The switch from the secular market to the Christian market entails sacrifices, especially for a successful romance writer. "The markets are completely different," Lori explains. A well-known romance author can count on a certain level of sales, and therefore income, in the general market. But it's never a given that the readers will follow an author into the new market. "You give up what you perceive to be security when you switch," Lori says. "You basically start over.

"But then it comes down to how much faith you have in God—do you really trust him. He will meet my needs—not every desire, but my needs—so I'm no longer afraid." Nor does her conscience bother her. She is free to write about her faith—and to *not* include explicit love scenes in her romances.

The letters keep coming, assuring her that somehow God is using her to bless others and show them something of God's love. "I feel so very humbled at being able to serve God in this way," she says. "Sometimes I get teary over the idea that God is alive and blessing *others* through someone like me.

"Sometimes our Father chooses the least likely candidate to

show what can be accomplished through his children with a willing heart. That's all he asks of us. He calls each of us to be willing to reach others through him. He can do great wonders through us. Whether it's in dynamic, dramatic ways, or in small, everyday ways, it's all important in God's kingdom work."

CHAPTER 6

Redeeming the Past

"True contentment is the power of getting out of any situation

all that there is in it."

— G. K. CHESTERTON

"In my fiction, I feel I need to allow my characters to cross bridges and earn the keys to what they want in life. They can't have everything they need on page one; they have to go through the fire, just as I have in my own life."

PATRICIA HICKMAN is an award-winning novelist and speaker. Her historical Australian series, LAND OF THE FAR HORIZON, garnered two Silver Angel Awards for Excellence in Media. Her other novels include *Voyage of the Exiles, Treasure Seekers, Katrina's Wings, The Touch, Sand Pebbles,* and *Fallen Little Angels.* She is the mother of three children, two on earth and one in heaven. She lives in North Carolina with her children and her husband, who is a pastor.

Flying Lessons

Patricia Hickman was born with an artistic bent. As a child she was always in front of an easel or writing poetry; as a teenager she added theater to the mix. "When I picked up my first Marguerite Henry books, I told myself, 'I'm going to grow up and write books like that.' That call never left me. Before Marguerite died, I was fortunate enough to correspond with her and tell her of the impression she left on me as a child."

But finding her voice as a writer did not come easily. She grew up in a sheltered small town called Russellville, in the Arkansas River Valley. Her family, bound by many emotional struggles, neither understood nor supported her artistic interests. Her parents had seen the failed marriages of their own parents. Her mother was determined to make her marriage to her father work, despite his infidelities. A complex man who had left a part of himself behind in the Depression, her father turned to volunteerism as an outlet, a way to feel useful after tuberculosis left his lungs too weak to return to work at a local dairy plant.

"His big heart and a desire to help the hurting left a big impression on me," Patricia says. "But he never extended that compassion to his own family. I watched the pain pass between my parents, a silent observer. My mother, my sister, nor I ever heard a word of encouragement or felt affection from him. For that I ached."

Patricia's father did not understand her artistic bent. "He hated that I was different from him, that I spent my days poring over books, writing, or sketching. He disparaged my creativity, telling me that I could never make a living as anything but a schoolteacher. Women had few choices, he felt."

Sometimes his anger erupted in unexpected violence. Usually

quiet and soft-spoken, he seldom raised a hand to Patricia or her sister, content to leave the discipline to his wife. But one day, when Patricia was about thirteen, father and daughter were sitting on the porch, simply chatting. Patricia says, "I answered him as always, nodding, agreeing with him, not understanding all of his deficient tales. He tended to ramble, but that didn't bother me. Suddenly Daddy flew into a rage and shouted, 'Don't you ever call me a liar!'" Her mother, hearing her husband's ranting, came out to the porch to find him jerking Patricia's arm, hitting her, throwing her down. "Defensive, Daddy accused me of 'jumping on him and attacking him.' Mama shook her head at me and said, 'Why do you have to stir him up?'"

It took a long time for Patricia to understand her father's problems. "Mental illness was never talked about nor acknowledged in those days," she says. "Although I once blamed my mother for not believing my story—that I did not provoke him—I've now come to understand that she never fully acknowledged my father's sickness. In her way of thinking, she had to believe him in order to maintain the peace, settle his rage, and keep their marriage intact. Mother used to wish for peace in our household above everything. But I had to find something deeper—forgiveness."

Hurting girls search to fill their voids in various ways. One Sunday Patricia wound up on a church bus bound for a Pentecostal church, a popular gathering place on Sundays in the valley. She sat alone most of the time. The preacher was a fiery sort, and every week Patricia listened to Preacher Parker pour out his heart about the love of Jesus Christ.

"One night," she says, "I did not go slowly into the arms of my Savior—I ran. I wept over a wooden altar and poured out my soul in prayer. God's presence was so strong that time escaped me. The bus driver ran his route and came back for me. He waited until a few minutes after midnight. I finally emerged, tear dampened and a new person."

Patricia's family did not take kindly to her conversion. Her father called her a fanatic. Her mother accused her of lying to her about being at the church so late. Her younger sister resented the fact that Patricia could no longer be drawn into a brawl. "The more I tried to share my good news with my family, the more they misunderstood me."

Things came to a head when Patricia applied to an out-of-state Bible college. She was eager to escape her family's instability and even more eager to accept the call on her life—she felt she belonged in the ministry. But when her father learned of her acceptance at Central Bible College in Springfield, Missouri, he grew violent once more. He made her cancel her admission to the college. He declared that she would attend the local college, and even chose her major—she would study elementary education. Girls had few choices, he felt. She would have to become a teacher and settle down in the valley.

"That was a real turning point for me, a bridge I had to cross in order to get a very important key," Patricia says. "I look at all the events of my life, all the difficult things, as bridges God has taken me across. At the end of the bridge, he gives me a key. And then one day, I arrive at this big door, and I know what I have to do. I realize I have picked up just the right keys to unlock that door."

Patricia took an English class taught by a local novelist. The teacher was an author who had published thirteen novels. Patricia was in awe of him. When he read one of her compositions aloud, a quietness settled over the class. The teacher asked, "What is your major?"

Patricia told him, "Elementary education."

"That's foolish!" he told her. "You're not a teacher; you're a writer!"

"That lit a fire in my soul," Patricia says. "I felt the Lord was showing me he was there all along." Even though it seemed impossible with her father's dictum, even though she kept her dream a secret, she did not let it die.

A young woman Patricia had known for years at her church approached her about starting a campus Chi Alpha, a Christian co-ed fraternity. She accepted the post eagerly. From the small core group

Patricia and her friend started arose a thriving campus ministry that is still in existence today. Patricia felt gratified by that. But she still struggled with the pain of her home life. She and a Christian friend rented a small one-bedroom house and became roommates. "Those were happy days. That sister in Christ became prayer partner and eventually my friend for life."

She met Randy Hickman one night after church. Randy had grown up in the church. He and Patricia fell in love, got married the next summer, and moved away from the valley in search of financial gain.

Almost a decade passed before the Hickmans would finally achieve the financial success they both sought. Patricia worked for a big corporation; Randy worked for NASA in a research firm. They had two children and struggled to overcome a mountain of debt they had accumulated early in the marriage. Overwhelmed with the cares of life, they both forgot God's earlier call.

"Early on, I blamed my struggles in life on my poor heritage, believing that if God had allowed me to grow up in a normal Christian family, I would have had better advantages, been accepted into a better circle of friends," Patricia says. "Then when my marriage failed to live up to my spiritual expectations, I could only conclude that God had led me away from his will. I felt that even he had rejected me. But it was simply another mask I wore. Just as I looked at my earthly father as one who continually prevented me from achieving my dreams, I blamed God in kind."

After becoming entangled in a war of politics within the company that employed her, Patricia's job was in peril. She felt bewildered; was God pouring out his wrath on her, as her father had done? Her staff hated her. She herself loathed what she had become—manipulative, grasping, blindly ambitious, arrogant.

It was another turning point, another bridge. "I was desperate to finally understand a life of full surrender to Christ. I wept and prayed. I studied God's Word, sought his voice in the midst of hating myself and all that I had become. One night I told the Lord that no matter what he did with me at that point, that I would live a life of full surrender regardless of my circumstances, regardless of how my spouse lived his life, but most of all, regardless of my past."

The next day a Washington, D.C., based firm offered her a better job. The more people-oriented firm also offered her twice the pay and a large staff. She accepted the job and changed her whole philosophy of management as she sought to live out her new surrender to God. "Serving Christ, I now realized, was a daily walk intended to touch others whose path I crossed. True servanthood had nothing to do with making a name for myself or leaving my mark on the world. Our business as believers is humankind, and the only mark we should leave is the gentle touch of Christ on people's hearts. And if they try to crush us, we're to leave behind nothing but his sweet aroma on their heel."

One day while sitting at her desk, someone laid a Christian magazine on her desk, a periodical called *Last Days Ministries*. The magazine was left in a co-worker's client's mailbox by mistake, and she thought Patricia might like to read it. Patricia opened the magazine and was immediately drawn to an article about sharing one's faith in Christ. "I wept and felt stirred. I knew once more that God was calling me into full-time service," Patty says.

At the same time, her husband was at his desk in a basement office at the NASA research firm. God spoke to his heart, as well, breaking his pride and turning him back to Jesus, just as he had done for Patricia. Then, through a Christian radio program, God also pricked Randy's heart for the lost. Randy confessed to his wife that he thought God was calling him into full-time ministry.

"We both wept and rejoiced," Patricia says. "Revival hit our home, and Randy established a family altar." He perused Bible college brochures while Patricia sought God's heart in her own prayer closet.

Randy attended Central Bible College while Patricia worked for a real estate firm. "This was the same college forbidden to me earlier by my father. You can't stop the hand of God." But another surprise cropped up. Thirty days after her employment with this Realtor, she shared an interesting bit of news with Randy—she was pregnant with baby number three.

After Jared's birth, Patricia grew to hate being away from home for eleven hours a day, grew to hate having a pager and having little time for her children. She was even angry at God: "Aren't you ever going to use me?" she railed at him. "But," she says, "I think God was just smiling. I hadn't picked up enough keys yet to open the incredible door that lay ahead."

It was partly because of her job that Randy both entered and departed Bible college debt-free. As soon as he accepted a position with a church in Baton Rouge, he turned to Patricia and said, "I have my dream; what's yours?"

"I want to be home with the kids, and I want to write novels. I want my writing to be used by the Lord." It seemed impossible.

She had saved all her pocket change in a knee sock. After six months she had saved $650—enough to buy a generic computer. She stared at the blank screen and realized she needed something else. She prayed for a mentor. Within two weeks a friend introduced her to bestselling author Gilbert Morris, who was starting a writers critique group. He asked her to join.

"I was petrified, so intimidated," Patricia says. "But I was desperate to learn." She drove around the block several times before she got up the courage to walk up to Gilbert's house and ring the doorbell for the first meeting. Nobody answered, so she went around to the backyard. Peering into the window, she spied Gilbert Morris asleep on the couch with a cat sleeping on his stomach! Bobby Funderburk, a fellow writer in the group, pulled up in his car and saw Patty peeping in at Gil. Bobby rang the doorbell again, and this time Gilbert answered. Patty says, "I didn't speak at those meetings for six months, I was so intimated!"

At those writers meetings Patty met Lawana Blackwell, another new writer, and the two became good friends.

Patricia was like a sponge, taking in all the feedback she could get, diligently applying it to her work. She sent out her proposals again and again, and received rejections—so many, she says, they were literally falling out of the mailbox. "I still keep those rejection letters in a file. They remind me of those closed doors that only God could open."

Gilbert Morris took her aside and advised her to change genres. The Christian market wasn't ready for contemporary, realistic novels, he said. So Patricia tried her hand at a historical series and sent out her proposal—three chapters and a query. In two weeks Bethany House called and said they wanted to buy her series. Three years into the series project, LAND OF THE FAR HORIZON, Patricia received two Silver Angel Awards for Excellence in Media.

But Patricia wasn't content just to get published. She felt a special call from the Lord to be a unique voice in the publishing world. There was a special story burning in her, a story borne out of her own pain. But she wrestled with sharing it. Would she be betraying her parents? Was the world ready for this kind of story? Was the time right now?

At a conference, she met Francine Rivers and confided in her. Francine said, "I think God wants you to write from the heart, to write your book of passion." Patricia cried all the way home. That night, she told God, "Lord, I don't know what you're trying to stir up inside of me; I'll have to rest in you." Just then, the words came: *Katrina's Wings.* The next day she sat down at her computer, prayed "Your will be done," and slowly, like a painful and wonderful birth, *Katrina's Wings* emerged.

Patricia needed every key she had collected to unlock the door that was *Katrina's Wings*—the pain of her childhood, the failures, the triumphs. "You will find a little of me in Katrina Hurley and a lot of my imagination in the rest of the story," she says. "God has shown me how to shine the light of Christ from out of a life of pain and glorify him in the process."

Her calling to write is wound up in her testimony of faith—"and I hope it always stays that way," she says. "Although I wandered around in such a miserable state for so many years, I see God's hand in even that—he used my pain and struggle to build his kind of character, shaping me so that I could stand as a tempered vessel, purified as only he can purify. I am wholly able to glorify him in every area of my life.

"I learn something new every day, with every rising of the sun," she observes. God shows up in the most remarkable places. For instance, Simba, her golden retriever, has a nasty habit of digging holes around the fence line of her backyard. To a gardener like Patricia, this is very annoying. But, she realizes, "he doesn't do it to break free from our one-acre yard. He does it just to satisfy his lust for digging."

One morning after it stormed, Patricia looked out of her kitchen window as usual, watching for the squirrels and birds. As the rain simmered to a soft, slushy mist, she noticed a robin on the ground near the fence line. "He was taking the most joyful bath," Patricia says. "He had discovered one of Simba's potholes in the midst of the dreary rain. The pretty male situated himself right in the middle of his newly found birdbath, a happy bather. I felt a sense of wonder when I saw the bright orange of his breast against the colorless morning. It was as though the sun had come up in a corner of our yard.

"Sometimes we feel that others come into our lives for the sole purpose of digging potholes, oblivious to the pain they leave behind. Sometimes we're guilty of spending too much time standing over those potholes, resentful, feeling victimized—woe is us! Those hurtful words that come out of nowhere wound us, tear tender flesh from our hearts, and bruise our spirits only to leave pits in our souls. And then, like a beautiful songbird, Jesus flies in. He takes one look at those rain-filled hollows while the thunder is still shaking our house. In the splendor of his bigness and Godness, he opens wide his wings, casting his soft cleansing rain around the perimeter of our pain—singing, healing us, and sweetening our sour countenance. He makes us grateful for the potholes in our gardens, the pain from our past. And we know that spring has once again come into our hearts. It smelled just like forgiveness that morning."

Patricia's desire is that all who hear her testimony or read her books will "know that the Lord is faithful to those who are willing to lay aside ambition, self-will, and bitterness of the past—faithful to finish the good work he has already started in your life. If you're having trouble finding your wings, lay aside your worries and trust in the only One who can make you fly—Jesus Christ."

"I'm here to wave a flag and say, 'The only way is Jesus, the only thing that makes sense is the Gospel, the only way out of the madness of the world is the cross.'"

LYNN MARZULLI lives in Malibu, California, and is a musician and composer who has recorded a number of albums. He has also researched in depth the topic of UFO cults, which became the basis for his novel *Nephilim* and its sequel, *Nephilim: The Unholy Deception*. Here he tells how he became such an expert in strange phenomena—and what God is doing with his expertise.

Redeeming the Darkness

As a young person, Lynn Marzulli had no use for God after the age of 13, when he stopped attending the Catholic church of his parents. When he was 18, his 16-year-old girlfriend was killed in an accident. Deeply affected by this, Lynn felt there was no God. He dabbled in drugs to ease the pain.

By the age of 21, he moved into the Philadelphia Ashram, which was part of the Divine Light Mission, Guru Maharaji's organization at that time. Lynn gave up all his money and possessions to the ashram, ate a strict vegetarian diet, was celibate, slept only five hours a night, and meditated morning and evening for an hour.

Though he'd left the church, he found himself drawn to other spiritual expressions, especially the New Age movement. His fascination with unusual phenomena drew him deeper and deeper into the supernatural and occultic world. By age 30, however, he realized something crucial: none of his experiences did a thing to change what was on the inside.

He read a book by Dave Hunt, *Cult Explosion,* and there was a little blurb included at the end about how to receive Jesus. Lynn said, "Jesus, if you're real, I want you to change who I am. I hate myself." Though at the time he didn't know what to call it, Lynn Marzulli knew there was something wrong with him on the inside, and he was sick of trying to change it on his own.

About a month later, he awoke from a dream, crying. Formerly repressed memories came to the surface, and Lynn went through a process of recalling them and getting free. A month after that, he began reading his Bible.

"The Lord began to take me out of the enemy camp," he realizes now. He got into a mentoring relationship with two men and quit dating for three years while he sorted out his spiritual life. He attended Bible studies and church services and slowly began to see his former experiences in terms of the Lord. He had indeed been in the enemy camp. Lynn knew firsthand that Satan is real and is in the business of deception.

Lynn's fascination with the enemy continued, but now from a whole new perspective. He sees the current fascination with UFOs and other unusual phenomena as tools that the enemy is using to deceive people. It bothered him that Satan was deceiving so many, just as he'd been deceived. He wanted to warn others about what was really happening and equip believers to share their faith with those who were caught up in supernatural phenomena.

Lynn had expressed himself creatively all his life through music (he composed piano pieces at the age of six) and writing (he started writing screenplays in high school). "When I read Frank Peretti's book *This Present Darkness*, I got serious about my own writing," he said. He wrote a novel, sent it out, and received "a couple of nibbles" but no contract.

By this time he had become fascinated by UFO "sightings" and began doing extensive research. "Most people have no clue as to what's going on with the UFO phenomenon," Lynn says. "It used to be so fringe, but now with *The X-Files* on television, there is this growing fascination with it. There are all kinds of Web sites, novels, and books coming out on it. Serious research is being done into alleged alien abductions; it's not just the stuff of supermarket tabloids."

Lynn's research has convinced him that serious spiritual deception is going on, and many people are falling under its spell. He wrote *Nephilim* to help believers and unbelievers alike understand the spiritual dimensions of the whole UFO culture, which he sees as part of the end times prophesied in Daniel and elsewhere in the Bible. "At the heart of all of this weird phenomena, whether you're talking about people who claim to have found the tomb of Jesus to those who believe in UFOs and alien abductions, is a negation of Jesus and what he did through the crucifixion," Lynn says. "Anything that negates the main work of Jesus—dying on a cross to save us from our sins—comes not from God but from the enemy." Through *Nephilim* and its sequel, Lynn sheds the light of biblical truth on the deceptions of our day. Though these ideas may seem fringe to many Christians, Lynn says that it's only because we don't realize how many people are caught up in them.

"One of the tactics of the devil is to introduce something, wait awhile, then reintroduce it," Lynn says. "The second time around, it doesn't seem so strange or bad. Look at what happened with the acceptance of abortion and the homosexual agenda. I think UFOs will be like that. Back in the 1950s, there was a lot of talk about them, and it all seemed very strange to most people. But now it seems more believable. We even have people like the Israeli journalist and skeptic Barry Chamish talking about the Nephilim—the giants mentioned in Genesis 6:4—returning to Israel. There are hundreds of UFO sightings weekly around the world. I think everything points to demonic deception on a growing scale."

Lynn sees his former involvement in the occult as the basis of his current calling: "Having my roots in the occult, then becoming a Christian—all I went through—has enabled me to look at this phenomenon from both an insider's view and a biblical view. I want to steer people away from getting involved and arm the Christian to know what to say to someone who is involved in the occult."

Lynn Marzulli is an example of a person whom God has redeemed and then sent back to those who are in the same bondage as he was. His years of wandering in the wilderness of the kingdom of darkness were not wasted. He didn't know it at the time, but God would use all those experiences, all that fascination with the occult, to equip him to be a beacon of light to other people.

Perhaps there are difficult experiences in your life that if surrendered to God could be used to pierce the darkness in another person's life. God likes to make beautiful mosaics out of broken pieces.

ROBIN LEE HATCHER

"I had to reach that place of understanding that success in my life is in knowing God more. It has nothing to do with how well a book is reviewed, or whether it wins a contest, or whether I ever sell another one again."

ROBIN LEE HATCHER, a RITA-Award-winning author, has written over thirty contemporary and historical novels and novellas. Her bestselling books have been published by WaterBrook Press/Random House, Silhouette Books, HarperCollins, Avon Books, and Leisure Books and will soon be published by Tyndale House, Zondervan Publishing, and Multnomah Publishers. There are nearly five million copies of her books in print in North America. Her books have also been published in nine other countries. One of her books, *The Forgiving Hour,* has been optioned for film. Robin is a past president/CEO of Romance Writers of America, a professional writers organization with over eight thousand members worldwide. In recognition of her efforts on behalf of literacy, Laubach Literacy International named the Robin Award in her honor. Robin and her husband live in Idaho.

No Compromise

Sometimes, in God's grace, the thing to which he calls us starts as his gift to us. That was Robin Lee Hatcher's experience when she began writing.

From the time she was in grade school, Robin was always a voracious reader and a compulsive writer. It wasn't until she was twenty-nine, however, that she even considered writing as a career. At that age, she was writing a newsletter for a horse association. As she says, "There are only so many articles you can write saying, 'Winter is coming, give your horse more grain.' You get tired of that." So Robin started writing more creatively, describing what her colts looked like running beside the mares in the snow. "That was probably the first spark," Robin says. "I did not realize at the time that it came from God, but I do now looking back. From the very beginning, he was orchestrating."

Robin began thinking about a story. She thought and talked for nine months. One day it hit her: It was time to quit talking and start writing. "I didn't know enough at the time to know I needed courage," she says with a laugh. She just sat down with her yellow legal pad and began writing. She wrote longhand in the evenings and on weekends, and she typed the manuscript at work during lunch hours and coffee breaks.

During that time, her life underwent much upheaval. After thirteen years of marriage, her husband began yet another affair, and the marriage crumbled and could not be saved. Her two daughters were ten and twelve. Suddenly she was a single mother, working full time to support her family.

Writing became her refuge. "To some degree, it was my place of safety," she says. "I had control over nothing else in my life, but I could control my writing. If someone misbehaves, you just press the delete key!" Writing also allowed her to work things through mentally. She could explore questions, including spiritual questions, in her books through character and plot.

One of the things Robin wanted to do was prove that a good story does not have to contain the coarse language and gratuitous sex scenes so common in the historical romances she'd read. When her first book sold, she felt God was honoring her intention by giving her a voice in the general market. She began writing in 1981, and her first book was published in 1984. When her ninth book was published, she quit her job to write full time. She's been writing ever since.

Her books sold well. As so often happens, success did not enhance Robin's relationship with God. It's not that Robin abandoned God. No, with most of us it's more subtle than that. She just began to compromise—a little here, a little there. Robin likens it to some forms of abuse. "If someone punches you in the eye, that's clear-cut abuse. But we may not recognize as abuse those nasty little words that cut and wound. I think compromise sneaks into our lives in the same way."

Robin had her lines drawn; she never took the Lord's name in vain, and she never wrote "what would be considered really sexy books." But "that does not alter the fact that I strayed from the path that I know I was originally set on. I regret that I ever sought success more than the pleasure of the Lord."

Of course, when Robin was compromising in her career, she was also making compromises in her spiritual walk as a whole. "I was single and making my own way, and there were many ways that I strayed." Not surprisingly, the awakening came through a crisis in her personal life, as God faithfully wooed back his wayward bride.

By that time Robin had remarried. A crisis in her marriage sent her "running to the foot of the cross, because there was no place else to find hope and strength," she says. "It was sort of a slap your forehead with the palm of your hand, 'duh!' moment where you think, *Why haven't I spent all my time here? This is the place to be.*"

After that point of crisis and repentance, God began to put new desires into Robin's heart, desires to serve God in new ways and to know him better. This eventually worked its way out in her career as well as her personal life.

Looking back, Robin can pinpoint some of the things that began to turn her around. In 1991 she read Francine Rivers' book *Redeeming Love*, which was originally published in the general market. "The book put the first spark in my heart of desire to write something with greater value than an entertaining read."

Robin met Francine in 1992, when Francine was working on her first book for the Christian market, *A Voice in the Wind*. The two writers spent hours talking. "That added fuel to my desire to serve God with my writing." Coupled with that was her frustration over her inability to include faith in her books for the secular market. In one book, toward the end, the heroine looks like she is dying in childbirth. Her husband, the hero, falls to his knees outside the house in the dark and prays. Just calls out to God, really, to spare her life; there is nothing about Jesus in his prayer. The editor cut the scene! She told Robin, "We don't want to offend any readers."

"I think that was the first nail in the coffin of my secular career," Robin says. "The worst pagan in the world will fall to his knees and pray in a crisis. Even if they don't say *God*, they cry out, 'Save my loved one.' I couldn't even include that in my books. Yet a few months later, another book was published by this same editor, and in that book one of the characters took Jesus' name in vain every time he opened his mouth. It didn't matter that that was offensive to Christians."

The desire to serve God in her career grew. But she didn't know exactly how. By this time, she was a recognized name in the romance book world. In fact, she was president and CEO of the Romance Writers of America from 1992 to 1994. In 1992, one of her books was a finalist in the prestigious RWA RITA Award (the romance world's version of the Oscars). One day at a women's retreat, a woman told Robin, "I believe that God took you to a place of visibility in the Romance Writers of America and in romance fiction, so that when you make the move to the Christian market, no one will miss it."

That turned out to be a prophetic word. In 1997, two editors from Christian publishing houses approached her and asked if she would like to submit a book proposal to their companies. "I knew this wasn't a move I could make simply because it would be another way to sell my books," Robin says. "In my deepest heart of hearts I knew this would have to be a call, that I would need to have a specific, undeniable word from the Lord. There are times in our lives when we know we're supposed to do something because the Scriptures tell us plainly. Other times we need that almost audible voice of God saying, 'This is the path, walk in it.' I had an offer on the table from a Christian publisher, but I could neither accept nor reject it until I heard from the Lord."

When the word came, Robin was in church, listening to a missionary from Sri Lanka. He spoke on Ephesians 2:10. After he quoted the verse, Robin suddenly knew that God was speaking to her heart, assuring her that he had prepared this career move in advance for his good purposes. He promised her that he would do far more than Robin could ever hope or dream, if she would follow him. "Then he added a caveat," she says. "He wanted me to be sold out, a hundred percent, to him. No little compromises. That was the moment that made every difference in my life, both personally and in my career."

Robin needed to trust that promise right away. Robin had sold her first book when only the opening scene was clear to her. The publisher had extended her a contract on the basis of a verbal conversation in faith that Robin could finish it. At three o'clock the morning after Robin accepted the offer, she woke in a cold sweat— "an all-out panic attack. I had never written either a contemporary or a Christian novel. All I had was the opening scene, given to me in a dream. I was too filled with panic to even pray. Now if I failed, I wouldn't just fail myself or the publisher, I'd fail God, too. It was terrifying."

Robin started reading her Bible. After some time, she came to

Isaiah 42:16: "I will lead the blind by ways they have not known, along unfamiliar paths I will guide them; I will turn the darkness into light before them and make the rough places smooth. These are the things I will do; I will not forsake them." Again, Robin felt God speaking to her. She was blind—she didn't know how she was going to write this book. She didn't know how it was going to end, or anything after the opening. But God knew, this was his book, and she did not have to be afraid. "I wrote that book in four months, without ever writing a synopsis or outline," she says. "I just tried to listen well and let God tell the story." That book was her first Christian novel, *The Forgiving Hour*.

Robin looks back on her journey with wonder at God's goodness. He gave her the talent and desire and opportunity to write in the first place. And even when she strayed, he faithfully and patiently drew her back to himself. In time, again with infinite patience, he showed her a better path for her career.

"Do I think it was God's perfect will that I wrote some of the books that I did that now make me cringe?" she says. "No. But I think he allowed me to follow the path that I did so that when he reawakened my desire to serve him in a new and better way, he could then turn the things that I had done to good."

Since she was so well known in RWA circles, she was able to send a copy of *The Forgiving Hour* to the entire RWA board of directors and all chapter presidents. "Because it was unique—my first hardcover, my first contemporary, my first Christian novel—many people read it who would not otherwise read a Christian novel," Robin says. She's heard from a lot of people, including those who are self-proclaimed atheists and people with no particular inclination toward faith, who said encouraging things about the book. "That was very exciting to me," she says. "In Isaiah it says that God's Word never returns void. Scripture figures prominently in that book, and God's voice, and I know that it's reaching hearts that would never pick up the Bible on their own. It's pretty awesome to be used by God that way."

One of the most gratifying responses to Robin came through an email from a woman who said she hadn't attended church in many years. When she read *The Forgiving Hour*, it caused her to realize it was time to start living for God and not for man. She opened her Bible for the first time in years. Robin says, "I just sat at my computer and wept. To think that God could change a life from something a puny person like me had done . . . that was unforgettable."

It's just such instances that keep Robin going, because changing her career to write exclusively for the Christian market has not been a perfectly smooth path. For one thing, it meant making less money than she was accustomed to. "We had just bought our house the year before I made this career move, and it had seemed like God had given us this house. But we had to take the stand that if God gave us this house, he also had the right to take it from us. That's where we lived, in trusting that God is in control. My husband and I—he had to be as committed to this as I was—determined that this was God's call, and there would be no turning back, no looking to the right or to the left."

God has proven faithful, providing for the needs of Robin and her family, and more than that, he's kept his promise to do far more than Robin could ever hope or dream. *The Forgiving Hour* has been optioned for film. Another one of her books, *Patterns of Love*, won a RITA Award in 1999. But through it all, God keeps Robin dependent on him, giving her just what she needs, not necessarily all she wants.

When the old temptations rear their heads—temptations to get hung up on bestseller lists or winning the latest award—she focuses again on the real question: "What is really important in the light of eternity? I had to reach that place of understanding that success in my life is in knowing God more. It has nothing to do with how well a book is reviewed, or whether it wins a contest, or whether I ever sell another one again."

Robin's career—along with the rest of her life—is on the altar. Isn't that where God wants each one of us? Only as we give everything to him, without reservation, is he able to mold the whole of our life to his good purposes. Purposes that will thrill and amaze us and cause us to fall on our faces in worship of the God who can work all things together—even our disobedience—for good, if we are called according to his purpose (Romans 8:28).

"I pray over everything I write. I ask God, 'What's the story supposed to say?' Then I see if it's saying it. I go over everything with a fine-toothed comb; I believe in excellence, in doing the best I possibly can. Then at that point, I leave the results up to God."

ANGELA ELWELL HUNT is the author of more than eighty books in nearly every genre imaginable, from nonfiction to fiction, from books for children of all ages (her award-winning *The Tale of Three Trees* has more than one million copies in print in sixteen languages), to adult nonfiction and novels. As a novelist, Angela has written historical fiction, prophetic fiction, contemporary, romance, and thrillers. A perpetual learner, Angela is constantly reading and learning and studying how to write better. The fact that many of her books have won awards attests to the level of excellence for which she strives.

Nothing Wasted in God's Economy

Some of us know early in life what we want to be when we grow up. And some of us stumble upon the path seemingly by accident, as a result of gentle proddings, influential people, and apparent coincidences. The path Angela Elwell Hunt is currently on was a result of the latter.

Angela never set out to become a writer. The closest thing to a "call" she can think of happened when she was in fifth grade at a summer camp. She was sitting outside beneath a tree during quiet time when she wrote these fateful words in her little booklet: "I think God wants me to become a poem writer." Even then, it was the result of a current influence. "I think that feeling had been impressed on my heart because our camp books included a lot of poetry. I remember something about, 'So if God decrees that a tree you will be, be the best little tree that you can be.' "

But after that incident Angela forgot all about writing until much later, when she was a junior in college. Because she had studied music and sang, everyone assumed she would become a professional singer. She even tried it. After two years of study at a community college, she toured for a year with the music group Re'Generation. The group did 530 concerts, and Angela learned firsthand what life as a professional musician would be. Was this really the kind of life she wanted for herself? Yes, she loved performing, but she also yearned for the comfort of hearth, home, and her books.

During their travels, the group was once snowbound in a blizzard for four days and nights. "It was serious stuff," Angela recalls. "All thirteen of us wrote about the event in our journals." When the director of Re'Generation, Pastor Derric Johnson, read Angela's entries, he said, "You know, you really have a way with words. When you go back to school, perhaps you should think of changing your major to English."

Angela realized that life as a full-time musician was not what she wanted for her future. "My voice was tired and my suitcase worn out," she says. So when she went back to school the fall of her junior year, she took Pastor Derric's advice and switched majors from music to English, with a minor in music. She was still on the road fifty percent of the time, since she was in college on a full music scholarship. But an English major was compatible with her lifestyle; she could read her books and write her papers while on the road.

Even though she switched majors, Angela says she wasn't thinking about writing novels. She thought she'd use her music and her talent with words to write musical plays for churches. But as opportunity would have it, as soon as she graduated from college she learned that a Christian school in town needed an English teacher. She applied and got the job. "It gave me another year to be immersed in literature," Angela says. "I loved the kids and enjoyed teaching, but after a year I knew it wasn't what I wanted to do long term."

For the next year she wrote curriculum for a large church in her area. She learned a lot about the whole process of producing printed materials, but after a year she decided she wanted a nine-to-five job with no pressure. She began working as a secretary to a man who is now a syndicated columnist. "I learned so much as I answered phone calls and typed up speeches and one of his manuscripts," Angela said. It piqued her interest in perhaps trying her hand at her own writing. But for two years, she was content to work this secretarial job while waiting for the babies to start coming.

When the babies didn't come, Angela and her husband, Gary, began adoption proceedings. And Angela did some hard thinking. She knew that when she got her baby, she wanted to stay home to care for him or her. "I'd worked too hard to get the baby, and I knew I wanted to be there to enjoy motherhood," she says.

Angela knew that staying home meant she needed some way to

bring in money. Writing seemed a good possibility. All along she had received encouragement from others about her writing. While still working as a secretary, her boss stuck his head into her office and said, "You know, I'll bet you could write us a good article about patriotism for the Fourth of July. Why don't you give it a shot?" She did.

"I kept telling myself that when the time was right, I would quit my job and become a writer," Angela says. "I finally decided that the time would be right when I plunged ahead and did it. At the time, I was thinking more about motherhood than about any sort of career. God nudged me forward, and I decided to send out business cards advertising my availability as a writer."

The baby came three months later. Angela wrote "anything people would pay me to write," mostly during nap times. She taught herself as she went along. "If an ad agency called and wanted me to write a radio ad, I'd go to the library and find a book about how to do it. I had no clue what I was doing, but as long as my clients seemed pleased, I figured I'd learn on the way." Within the first year she was contributing as much financially working three hours a day as she had while working eight hours a day in her other job. The best part was, she says, "I had my baby to love and care for, and that's where my fulfillment lay."

For five years Angela did freelance writing for magazines, businesses, and ad agencies. Then in 1988, she saw an ad for a *Writer's Digest* contest for unpublished children's authors. She got a book out of the library on how to write a picture book, followed the formula as best she could, and got a friend to illustrate it. She won the contest, and suddenly Angela Hunt was a published author!

At the same time, Angela wanted to share with others what she had learned from her own experience about the adoption process (by then they had adopted two children). So she wrote a book about adoption and sold it to a publisher. Those books gradually moved her out of writing for periodicals and into the book publishing industry. Because her husband is a youth pastor ("he calls me the pastorette because I'm so involved"), she began to write fiction for middle-schoolers. Then an editor suggested she write adult fiction, and she did. Now she writes mostly fiction but also does other publishing projects that might come her way.

Angela stresses that for her, writing has been a career God has provided for her to make a living and be involved with her children and her husband's ministry in the way she wants. "I'm very pragmatic," she says. "I was part of a writer's panel and someone asked, 'What motivates you to write?' And my first honest answer is, 'To pay the mortgage.' For me to discount that I write primarily to make a living would be to knock every Christian who goes to work as a dentist or a secretary or whatever. We all have jobs to do that are God's provision for us to make a living. Mine just happens to be with words. We all have something that God calls us to do, and we're all called to do it with excellence—whatever it is."

That's where the "ministry" comes in—when we do our work with excellence. Angela always worked very hard to learn her craft, and then to hone it, to give it everything she has. "Pastor Derric always taught us to work as if everything depends on you, and to pray as if everything depends on God." This twin approach—hard work and prayer—should be the hallmark of any endeavor attempted by a Christian. Then, Angela says, it's God who gives the results.

Results need to be left in God's hands because they are unreliable barometers of success. Results for an author are measured in sales figures and readers' responses. But neither of those give a true picture. An author may think she's written the best book possible, and it doesn't sell well. Or maybe a book that didn't seem so good really takes off. The process can be discouraging if success is the focus. "We all labor over our books," Angela says. "While we're writing, the characters fill our thoughts, our dreams, and every waking moment. Then the book is sent off to the editor and publisher, where it may be 'in process' for up to a year. Then when the book comes out, we are impatient, we want it to be met with great fanfare and appreciation, and often we hear silence. That's when I have to trust that God knows what he is doing and is taking the book to the lives who need it."

Even when an author does hear from a reader, the response isn't always a reliable indicator of whether she was successful in following God's direction for a particular book. Angela remembers a letter a reader sent to her publisher. The reader felt that Angela's book—which happened to be her first adult novel—was too harsh and brutal and unfit for children. "How could a Christian write such things?" the reader had asked.

At first Angela felt devastated. She had prayed very hard about that book, as she did for every book, and had written it the way she felt God wanted her to. Did she misread God? Eventually she realized that she had given God lots of opportunities along the way to correct her if she was going astray. No, this was the story God wanted her to write. She needed to receive this criticism the way she'd learned to receive criticism as a pastor's wife: listen, prayerfully discern if there is even a kernel of truth in it, learn from that, and then move on. "I write to please God (he's my coauthor) and the majority of my readers," she says.

Looking back, Angela can see that no experience of hers was ever wasted. Life on the road taught her to strive for excellence and pointed her away from music. Each of her jobs, her life experiences such as adopting two children, being the wife of a youth pastor, even her financial needs, were tools God used in the process of making her a writer. "Every struggle I've had I've been able to turn into a book somehow," she says, adding, "I think that happens for everyone, not just writers. God uses everything for our good, to help us fulfill what he has for us to do in the world, and to shape us into the image of Christ."

CHAPTER 7

Obedient to One Voice

"It is within my power either to serve God or not to serve him.
Serving him, I add to my own good and the good of the whole
world. Not serving him, I forfeit my own good and deprive the
world of that good, which was in my power to create."

— LEO TOLSTOY

"My reason for writing fiction is to tell a story. I do not consider myself so much a 'Christian writer' as a Christian who writes. My struggle is to write what's true and right and not what's pious. The call I feel is not to write for Christians per se, but to write for people who read fiction, and to write in such a way that they will be touched by God's truth, whether they expected it or not."

PATRICIA SPRINKLE writes murder mysteries—straight whodunits with clues and an ending in which the murderer loses and truth triumphs once more. Some people are surprised that a Christian would write murder mysteries, but Patricia has published seven in the SHEILA TRAVIS series and three in the MACLAREN YARBROUGH series. In addition, she wrote *The Remember Box,* a memoir novel about growing up in North Carolina in the early days of the Civil Rights struggle, and its sequel, *Carley's Song,* about a girl learning about love during the era of the Korean War. She has also published several nonfiction books, including *Women Who Do Too Much, Children Who Do Too Little,* and *Women Home Alone.*

Embracing the Joy

Patricia Sprinkle didn't decide to be a writer. By ninth grade she realized she *was* a writer already. In doing a report on professions (she had to choose between writer, mortician, and farmer), she chose to research the writing profession. She learned that writers are people who tell stories. "I realized that's what I did—I'd tell myself stories when I went to bed," Patricia says.

In high school, a guidance counselor gathered thirteen students who liked literature and started a literary magazine. "She spurred me to believe that I could do whatever I wanted. It was her belief in us that made us believe in ourselves." She chose Vassar College because of its strong creative writing department. By this time she had become a Christian and was seeking God's direction.

Her parents gave her the option of staying with them for a while after college to save money so she could fulfill a dream—to go to Scotland for a year. In the fall of 1966, Patti went to Scotland, having no idea where she was going. But God was leading.

"On the train one day I heard two students talking about Braemar. I went to that village and lived there, and received affirmation after affirmation that I was where God wanted me." For example, when one of the women in the village burned her hand badly, Patti was able to go and wash dishes for her. When the girl who was to direct the Christmas play emigrated to New Zealand suddenly, Patti helped direct the play.

While she was in Scotland, Patti strongly felt God's call to write. In Braemar she met Martha Duncan, who became her mentor. "She said to me, 'Why don't you write for Christians since you are a Christian?' And I said to her, 'Why don't you write short stories?' Eventually, Martha ended up writing stories, and I was writing for the church." Patti's first works were published in Scotland: one short story, one short play, one article interview, and one poem. "It didn't help me know what to focus on," Patti says, "but it was exciting to get the acceptance."

After she had been in Scotland for a year, she moved to the United States and found a job in Atlanta, editing trade publications. She hated it. When she left there, she worked for the national offices of the Presbyterian Church doing research and writing, and stayed five years. That job gave her many valuable skills: she learned to edit, she learned to meet deadlines, and she discovered her gift for public speaking. But she wasn't writing fiction.

She was, however, reading lots and lots of mysteries. After she married, her husband said, "Why don't you write a mystery to pay for all the ones you read?"

"I knew immediately the first one I would write," she says. And so she began. But two groups opposed her. She was working for the Presbyterian Hunger Program, and those who shared her passion for the poor told her it was a waste of time to write mystery novels when she could be doing more for hungry people. Another group of Christian friends didn't think writing murder mysteries was a worthy pursuit at all for a Christian. "One person even told me it was demonic to write about murders," she recalls, wincing.

Patti listened to those voices for six years and shelved the work that she really wanted to do. She was miserable. "One day in tears I said to God, 'I want to write murder mysteries.' And I got this sense that God was saying that even if I didn't write them on earth, I would in heaven. That comforted me tremendously."

Her husband asked, "What would it take for you to write a mystery? You were so happy when you were working on that book." Patti thought and said, "I would need to visit Chicago in February to get the feel and smells right." That was the setting of the novel she had started.

Shortly after that, her husband, a pastor, got a call to move to Chicago. Patti felt that maybe this was God's call to her, as well. They did go and stayed there for five years. Once the first mystery was finished, Bob encouraged Patti to go to a mystery writers conference. All the way to the conference, Patti felt that God was telling her, "Go up there and serve." No matter what she tuned in to on the radio or read, all she kept hearing about was serving. She thought she was going to the conference to find an agent and learn more about publishing, but God kept telling her to serve.

At the initial reception, Patti noticed it was just like a high-school dance, with the popular people in the middle and the others around the edges. Patti went around the edges getting to know folks. In so doing, she met a woman whose sister was a writer. As they made plans to have breakfast together the next morning, someone behind Patti said, "Breakfast! That sounds good!" The woman turned out to be a well-known writer Patti greatly admired. Patti and her new friend ended up having breakfast with two well-known authors. Afterward, one of the authors introduced Patti to her agent. "That agent didn't normally take on new writers, but he became my agent anyway," Patti says. She marvels at God's faithfulness when she was willing to obey and follow his direction, even if she didn't understand it.

Patti continued to step out in faith in the direction of her heart's desire—to write mysteries. And God opened doors. Once she gave herself permission to write fiction, though she was incredibly busy, she was also very happy. She still worked full time on the hunger project, but she found time to write, as well. Her job required lots of travel, so she lugged along a big portable computer and wrote much of her third mystery in hotel rooms. She worked days and evenings, but was strict about taking time off for Sabbath rest. "You don't get as much done when you work seven days a week," she says. Patti arranges her life so she doesn't even cook much on Sundays. After worship, Sunday afternoons are a time to rest, recreate, and refuel.

She wrote both fiction and nonfiction, and taught workshops. Her books got published. The bills got paid. And Patti found a deep sense of fulfillment. "It's strange," she muses. "For six years I didn't write fiction, though that was what I really wanted to do. I took any other kind of assignment that came up, just to help pay the bills. And it was a struggle in every way, including financially. But then when I started writing fiction, things began to work out. Again and again, when I choose to do what I truly believe I need to be doing instead of listening to what all the voices around me are saying, God is incredibly faithful in confirming that this is what I need to be doing."

Learning to listen to God's voice has been an ongoing process, with tests all along the way. Sometimes she feels impeded from writing a story the way she feels it should be written because of certain strictures of the so-called Christian marketplace. For instance, she may need a character to use a certain word that Christians don't normally use. Not using that word may well keep it from being the story she feels led to write.

"I am a writer who is a Christian," she says. "I feel as a Christian, I have to deal with the darkness of the world as well as with the light. All of Scripture talks about the darkness. If the darkness is not written about truly, then the Gospel cannot be seen in all its glory." The good news of salvation doesn't make sense if there's no need for salvation portrayed, if characters are always good apart from Christ.

Even during the moments of trial, Patti has found God faithful. When she hit one particular stricture—she needed a character to attend a cocktail party but knew that would offend some of her publisher's customers—she turned to a project that had been on her heart to write for a long time. She wanted to write about where she grew up and about her father, as a gift to him. She called her publisher and said, "For some reason, I can't seem to write this mystery. But I have another book idea; can I write that one instead?" And that is how *The Remember Box* came to be written.

Since *The Remember Box* is not a mystery, it represents a departure for Patricia Sprinkle. But that, she has found, is what God often does—he leads into new territory. We may want to stay on the sure path, the safe way. But Jesus shook people up with his stories, his actions, and his life. He especially shook up the religious leaders.

Patricia Sprinkle finds that God is not at all shy about shaking people up. His way may be riskier, but it's also freer and full of joy. "My husband preached once on the verse 'the joy of the Lord is your strength' (Nehemiah 8:10). It's not my joy that keeps me going—it's God's joy in what I am doing as I follow him; that's what gives me strength."

If you find yourself blocked and uncertain as to what to do, could it be that the voices of other people are drowning out the voice of the Lord? Is God asking you to take a step of faith in a direction others may not understand? The choice is yours. There's safety on one side but on the other, freedom and joy beckon.

BODIE THOENE

"My calling is to tell stories like Jesus did—parables about people's lives. I seek to take a God's-eye view of history and show how the Lord is infused in all of history. If you leave out God, I believe your stories will be two-dimensional rather than three-dimensional."

BODIE THOENE has written numerous novels, many with her husband, Brock, and has won eight Gold Medallion Awards for historical fiction. Her first book, *The Gates of Zion,* was published in 1986, at a time when very little Christian fiction was being published. She is one of the pioneers who opened the fiction market in Christian publishing. Her books in the ZION LEGACY and ZION CHRONICLES series, and *Shiloh Autumn* are among the top five requested in libraries.

Despite Disability

Most people who end up as successful authors read voraciously from an early age. This was also true for Bodie Thoene, whose mother read books to her from the time she was a preschooler. "I never owned a Dr. Seuss book," Bodie says. "My mother read to me books *she* wanted to read, everything from Dickens to Walter Farley. And I loved it."

Then Bodie got to school and discovered a potentially devastating fact: she couldn't read. "I couldn't make my eye connect with the printed word," Bodie says. Back when she was a child in the fifties and sixties, dyslexia was not a well-known disability. She didn't know why she couldn't read or do math. School became a struggle.

But her mother knew her child was not stupid, she just needed some help. In third grade, she hired someone to work with Bodie. She continued to read to Bodie, who would let the words wash over her like water to cleanse and soothe her soul. Though Bodie could not read the words with her eyes, she heard them with more than her ears. Her disability taught her to hear with her heart.

In seventh grade, her mother enrolled her in a journalism class. When she was sixteen, she decided she wanted to work on the staff of a newspaper. She studied the paper and noticed that there was no column addressed to young people. Bodie dressed up, entered the editor's smoky office, and told him, "I notice you don't have anyone covering the high school. I'd like to do it." He hired her, paying fifty cents a column inch, and that began her career as a professional writer.

Here she was a writer, and still she couldn't read or do math. Intelligence tests said she was smart, yet she got through school only with great difficulty. People said she was not living up to her potential. She felt like "a dumb, undisciplined person."

But she got to college, and there two key words lifted the great burden of her distorted self-image. She heard the word *dyslexia* for the first time; now there was a name for her condition, and she discovered others shared it. She asked if she could tape her classes instead of taking notes. The *yes* to that request opened the way for Bodie to compensate for her problem and move on.

Move on she did. She worked for *U.S. News & World Report* in college. Having grown up in a family that talked, lived, and breathed politics, with a father who was Jewish, she became fascinated with the history of Israel. Her mother became a Christian, and one day Bodie attended a lecture with her on prophecy. She realized that the only way to explain the birth of the nation of Israel was God. She studied prophecy and realized that Jesus was the fulfillment of biblical prophecy. Her decision to receive Jesus as her personal Lord and Savior was mostly intellectual then: "This was truth, and I decided I would embrace it."

Bodie married Brock Thoene, "whom I had known always; we grew up a couple of blocks from each other." She and Brock would go together on freelance writing assignments. Once she wrote a book called *The Fall Guy* with Chuck Roberson, John Wayne's stunt man. John Wayne read the book and loved it and hired Brock and Bodie to write for Batjac Productions. There they began to perfect their craft. Once John Wayne told Bodie, "You can tell people what they need to hear, what you want them to hear. But you gotta put it in a good story." She mulled over his words and realized he was talking about the principle of parable. It's what Jesus did: he couched in story some hard truths that people may not have received in any other way.

Another time Bodie was walking down the hall, and John Wayne stopped her and asked, "What's your dream, Bodie? What do you want to do more than anything else? What is your 'Alamo'?" Bodie knew that John Wayne's dream was to do a movie on the Alamo—a dream he had carried around with him until he fulfilled it at age forty. Bodie asked herself, *What in all of history excites me?* The answer: the story of the rebirth of the nation of Israel. "You gotta do it," Wayne told her. "It's the Jewish Alamo."

Meanwhile, Brock and Bodie had children—three in all. It was in holding her first child for the first time that Bodie added a new dimension to her faith. "I was an intellectual Christian at the time," Bodie explains. "As I held our daughter, I looked at Brock and said, 'What if God did something to her to teach me a lesson?' Brock said, 'God loves her more than you do. That's not what God is like.' All of a sudden the Lord spoke to my heart and said, 'It's not how much you love me, but how much I love you. *I* gave my child for you.' Then my heart was fused with what my head already believed."

Eventually God put her to the test to act on her faith. "God spoke to me when I was sitting on a rock in the mountains one afternoon," Bodie says. She and Brock had already left their lucrative jobs at Batjac Productions because they felt they needed to be more available to the children. "But," she says, "I was worried about everything—would we make it?" The answer was from Matthew 6:33, "Seek first his kingdom and his righteousness, and all these things will be given to you as well." She sensed the voice of God in her heart saying, "You already know you can make it in the secular market—because you did. So the question is, whom will you serve and *how* will you serve?" Was she willing to turn her talents toward filling the deep hole that existed in the Christian market, where almost no fiction was available?

She wrote her book about the rebirth of Israel, and Bethany House published *The Gates of Zion*. It won a Gold Medallion from the Evangelical Christian Publishing Association, and turned out to be the first of more than thirty novels. The many years that she and Brock spent honing the craft of writing and the passion she feels about the power of words and of story slowly coalesced into a calling to write fiction that speaks of God's ways not only to the churched, but to the unchurched, as well.

It's a calling she shares with Brock, her partner in every sense of the word. She still has great difficulty with reading, so Brock reads to her. He reads books, he reads the fan mail, and he reads back what she writes so that her finely-tuned ear can detect the errors. Brock, the historian, does the research.

"I liken writing a book together to building a house," Bodie says. "Brock lays the foundation and puts in the plumbing and electricity. I decorate, hang the wallpaper, put the people and furniture in." Brock also monitors her energy level, and when she's overworked, he firmly suggests a break. "He takes care of me the way a lover should while he helps me carve the book," Bodie says. "We've been married for more than thirty years, and I feel like a teenager, I'm so in love with him," Bodie says.

Though to this day Bodie Thoene has great difficulty with reading, it has not stopped her from fulfilling a call to reach people with the truth and love of God and show his hand in history. God has supplied all she ever needed: supportive parents ("they made all the difference"), alternative means to do her studies, opportunities, and a supportive husband and children.

Confirmation of this call comes not so much through the awards her books have garnered, but in the letters from readers. "I think of the Jewish man who read *Jerusalem Vigil* and said it was like his own life was flashing before his eyes. He's not a believer, as far as I know, but our books have made a difference in his life. The calling is confirmed when the lonely people in the world who read the books in whatever language say, 'Through your words I heard the Word of God sing to my heart, and it changed me forever.' Then what we're doing is not just craft, or even a faith, but giving a cup of cold water to a thirsty person. Then it is offering what I know and what I do and letting all the things in my life combine to the service of Christ and eternity."

What service can you render so that the Word of God can awaken someone's heart to God's love song? There are so many thirsty people in the world . . . and so many ways to offer a cup of cold water.

TERRI BLACKSTOCK

"With every book I write, I strive to make it strong enough to touch people, to change them. It's a real passion with me. My calling is to challenge Christians. I was such a lukewarm Christian for so long, I want to wake others up and inspire them to bear fruit."

TERRI BLACKSTOCK, writing under two different names, was an award-winning romance novelist writing for publishers such as HarperCollins, Harlequin, and Silhouette, with thirty-two published books and 3.5 million books in print. In 1995, she began publishing novels in the Christian market, under her own name, Terri Blackstock. She has written several series published by Zondervan, including THE SUNCOAST CHRONICLES, SECOND CHANCES, and NEWPOINTE 911. She also wrote the novella *Seaside* and coauthored two books with Beverly LaHaye: *Seasons Under Heaven* and *Showers in Season.*

Waking Up

Terri Blackstock was the daughter of a couple of married teenagers; her mother was fifteen and her father eighteen when she was born. Her father became a fighter pilot in the Air Force, and the family moved every few months. Terri turned to her imagination to entertain herself and assuage the loneliness of not being able to forge lasting friendships.

Her mother, who'd been raised Southern Baptist, made sure Terri and her two siblings went to church wherever they happened to live. Her father, an agnostic, rarely attended. When he was sent to Vietnam, Terri prayed for him often. She began writing poetry. When he returned, Terri's parents divorced, and she rarely saw her father.

Terri turned to writing to make sense of her turbulent emotions. When she was twelve she wrote a short story in poetry form about a little girl whose older brother was killed in Vietnam. "It was a tearjerker but very therapeutic for me," Terri says.

It also gave her her first taste of what it felt like to be a published author. Her mother sent the story off to the local newspaper, the *Clarion-Ledger* in Jackson, Mississippi, and they published it. "Seeing my own work in print set writing in my heart, and I decided right then and there that I was going to be a writer when I grew up," she says.

Two years after that, through the death of a schoolmate from a car accident, Terri began to think deeply about spiritual matters for the first time. "I took my broken heart to Christ and gave it to him, along with my life. It was the first time I had felt intimately connected with my Lord and Savior and the first time I understood exactly what he had saved me from," Terri says.

For a couple of years Terri continued to walk closely with God. But then her youth group at church fell apart, and she drifted into friendships with several unbelievers. In her senior year of high school, she began dating one of these friends.

After high school, Terri attended a community college. Her father was supposed to provide for her college education, but her parents couldn't agree on how much or when it was to be paid. "I quickly became frustrated at the ongoing fight between my parents over the money," Terri says. "In my second semester, I switched my major from journalism to secretarial science because I had decided that college was not worth the fight." After her freshman year, she went to work full time as a secretary. At the age of eighteen, she moved out of her mother's house and rented an apartment. At twenty, she married her unbelieving, unchurched boyfriend.

They moved to Monroe, Louisiana, and started working their way through Northeast Louisiana University. With the help of student loans and their jobs, they kept from having to depend on their parents for college money. "Working my way through college created a fierce intensity in me," Terri says. "I didn't want to waste a dime of my hard-earned money, so I took my studies very seriously." She majored in English and studied the masters of literature so she could become a better writer.

When she graduated from college, Terri immediately began looking for a way to break into the publishing world. She joined a group of romance writers who met monthly in Shreveport. "I had no interest in writing romance, because in college we had all turned our noses up at genre fiction," Terri says. "I had dreams of writing the Great American Novel."

But as she got to know those women and began to read their work, she realized that some of them were very skilled writers. "The books were not sappy melodramas as I had believed, and I found that I enjoyed reading about relationships of all kinds." Terri decided to try to write a romance novel.

Knowing that most romance novels contained explicit sex, Terri looked for a way not to compromise her Christian beliefs. "I told myself I was only going to write what is called 'sweet romance'—romances without sex or profanity," she says. When Silhouette accepted her first novel, *Blue Fire*, she was ecstatic. She was finally a published author. She had arrived!

But the second sale didn't come as easily as the first. While her friends in the writers group were making lots of money, she was left behind. As she continued collecting rejection slips and wrote her second, third, and fourth novels, she began to feel competitive, ambitious. "I realized that my market was much more limited than theirs because I refused to include sex scenes," she admits.

So she began to compromise. She included a little more sensuality than she had before—and suddenly sold a book to Harlequin. She added a little more sex to one of the two books she was still trying to market. "I justified it to myself by saying it was between a husband and wife," Terri says. That book sold also to Silhouette. "Feeling quite successful and telling myself that the Lord would not allow these to sell if he didn't want them to, I included even more sex in the next book, and these characters were not married." That book sold to Dell. She had finally arrived—three books with three publishers who were all interested in more.

"I felt very successful," Terri says. "But success didn't bring me happiness, because I was a Christian, and the Holy Spirit I was grieving was making me miserable." At the time Terri didn't recognize the Spirit's voice. She fell into the trap of believing that more money and more published books would make her happier. She began working twelve hours a day at the computer. She turned out four books a year. By 1986, she had six books out under her own name, Terri Herrington, and her pen name, Tracy Hughes. "Writing consumed me," Terri admits. "But happiness didn't come."

Still blind to the true nature of her unhappiness, Terri decided that the stigma of writing romance novels was what kept her from true contentment. She began working on a "mainstream novel," and sold *Her Father's Daughter*, a modern-day *King Lear* story, to HarperCollins. "I had now hit the big leagues of publishing," Terri says. "But I still had no happiness because the books contained worldly plots and illicit sex and even a good bit of profanity."

She sold several more books to Harper and continued writing for Harlequin and Silhouette. She was very busy, and the royalty checks poured in.

During all this time, Terri still actively attended her church. She made sure her two daughters never missed a service on Sunday or Wednesday nights, and she even began teaching a Sunday school class for three-year-olds. "I compartmentalized my career, as if writing romance had nothing to do with my spiritual life," she says. "Sometimes I would sit in church and get convicted that what I was doing was wrong," she says. "It would make me very uncomfortable, but then I'd walk out into the light of day and shake that conviction from my mind."

Terri had the fine art of self-deception mastered. "I told myself constantly that I wouldn't be that successful if God wasn't opening these doors for me. I told myself that I wasn't hurting anyone and that these books were just harmless entertainment. I told myself that I couldn't help how my characters behaved—it wasn't reflective of who I was. I repeated those thoughts to myself like some sort of mantra. They replaced prayer in my life."

Terri eventually realized she never prayed. Her Bible remained in the car, handy for carrying to church on Sunday. "I did not hunger for righteousness," she says. "Instead, I hungered and thirsted for more money and more recognition."

She had been giving interviews and talking about her writing career. When her local paper, the *Monroe News Star*, decided to do an article on her, she said yes.

This reporter was no different from the rest; he wanted to talk about sex and money. Terri tried to steer him to other parts of her life, telling him of her church work and the children she taught in Sunday school. She says she figured the reporter would balance the story of "the demure woman who writes erotic romance with the church lady who is the pillar of the community."

The article came out in the Sunday newspaper, and suddenly her two worlds collided. As she was getting ready for church, her husband brought the paper in and read her the first line: "Terri Herrington has no trouble weaving tales of sex and romance in her novels, but she never sweats in church."

"I was just mortified, too mortified to go to church that morning," Terri says. She again heard the voice of the Holy Spirit, telling her something was wrong here. If she felt this mortified when what she was doing was brought into the light, something was not right. Between Sunday and Wednesday, she agonized over what would happen when she went back to the church to teach her class. Would a committee meet her at the door and declare her too brazen to teach their children? Would the pastor call her into his office for a heart-to-heart talk?

None of her fears materialized. In fact, the associate pastor met her in the hall, hugged her, and said he was proud of her. Other people congratulated her that night. But her conscience was pricked. "Deep in my heart, I knew that the Lord wasn't congratulating me, but I didn't have the faith or the sensitivity to the Holy Spirit to give up my writing."

When her husband turned thirty and became restless, they sold his small business and moved to Safety Harbor, Florida. For much of the time after that, he was unemployed. Though guilt gnawed at Terri, she told herself that her family depended on her income. She didn't feel she had the option of quitting.

In fact, she felt she needed to work harder than ever. The tension on her marriage finally led to divorce. Now she had two daughters, ages eight and three, to raise herself. Rather than turning to God, she went to a psychic for direction. The psychic told Terri her marriage was over and to do whatever she could to take care of herself.

She moved back to Mississippi with her children, renting an apartment. She worried about making a living while she was mired in depression. But the Lord was at work. "He gave me several very sweet signs that he had not forsaken me, even though I had forsaken him," she says. "He gave me a Christian neighbor who was also divorced with two children the same ages as my own. She helped me nurse my wounds and pointed me back to God."

When Terri took her eight-year-old, Michelle, to a family counselor to help her deal with her anger, the Christian counselor told Terri *she* was the one who needed counseling. One night Michelle heard on the radio about a divorce recovery seminar being offered at a local Baptist church, and Michelle encouraged Terri to go. She swallowed her pride and went.

After the seminar was over, some of the attendees moved into a divorce support group. When Terri was on her feet again, she quit attending, but by then she was firmly entrenched in this church home.

Still writing romance, she began to come under deep conviction that she was not pleasing the Lord. She tried to clean up her act by writing less explicit love scenes, but she still knew she needed to quit. "I sought the counsel of men rather than the Lord," she admits. "My family counselor suggested that I didn't need any more major changes in my life for a while, and I certainly didn't need the stress of uncertainty about how I was going to support my kids. Others suggested that I shouldn't quit because I had such a huge readership. 'Think how many people are touched by your writing,' they said."

In her heart Terri felt that God was asking her to do something else: repent. She knew repentance meant making a change. But what kind of change was the Lord asking of her?

Terri started trying to balance out the sex with some sort of faith message. "But it was watered down and had little impact," she says. "I guess the small effort salved my conscience for a while, though, because I once again ignored the conviction and kept writing."

She met and later married Ken Blackstock, who appeared to be a godly, churchgoing man. Soon she discovered he was not what he appeared. The marriage didn't seem to be working.

One year into their marriage, in 1993, Ken tuned in to a Christian radio station. He drove a lot in his job, and usually listened to rock stations, but he kept turning back to the Christian station, listening to a pastor's messages. After a few days, he was so overcome with conviction that he pulled over to the side of the road. He lowered his head against the steering wheel and wept, then he repented of the life he had led.

When Terri saw the changes in her husband, she grew even more uncomfortable with herself. "I began to see him bear fruit, and it reminded me how far I had fallen. In the beginning of my Christian journey, I, too, had been that zealous. I hungered to become closer to God myself."

Many people were praying for her, though Terri didn't know it then. Finally the conviction became so strong that she couldn't deny it any longer. "One day, I finally got on my knees and told the Lord that I never wanted to write another word that didn't glorify him. I confessed my fear, and I told the Lord that if he never let me write again, that would be fine. I would trust him."

Terri had finally repented. "It was as if God held my hand and said, 'Now I can help you.'"

She would need all the help she could get. Repentance did not make her problems go away. She was committed to write several more books. How could she get out of those contracts? Also, there was her agent to consider. How could she tell her agent—who by now was also a close friend—that she had decided to quit writing romances?

Terri found that trust in the Lord is never disappointed. One day out of the blue, her agent called to tell Terri she was leaving the business. After a moment of stunned silence, Terri began laughing. She told the agent of her own plans. The agent was amazed that they had come to the same decision at the same time. But Terri was beginning to realize that she had recommitted her life to a God who answered prayer.

Terri decided the only way to get out of her writing contracts was to just tell her publishers what she wanted to do. One of the editors set up a conference call. Her editors tried to talk her out of quitting—she was just suffering from burnout or mid-life crisis, they said—but she remained firm. She told them this was a spiritual decision, that this was what she felt God wanted her to do.

They finally agreed to let her out of all but one of her contracts, if she paid back the advance. She agreed—another big step of faith. It would mean she'd have to trust God to provide the money, since she had been living on it for the past year. In the end, it turned out that her previous books had sold well enough that Harlequin owed her more money than she owed them. Again, the Lord had answered her prayer.

The one book she had still contracted for was part of a series she had agreed to write with two very close friends. "Because I didn't think my decision needed to impact them financially, I told them that I would go ahead and write that book, but it had to glorify God, and it would not have any sex or profanity whatsoever," Terri says. "They agreed, and Harlequin published it that way." (Some would call that another miracle!)

Now all she needed was for a Christian publisher to open its door to her. "I knew that my background might make me poison to any of the Christian publishers," she says. Not to mention the fact that she was good at writing contemporary stories, and most of what was published in the Christian market at that time was historical fiction, westerns, and prairie romances.

One day while on a cruise, she noticed that almost everyone on board was reading some type of suspense novel. "I started talking to the Lord about the idea of giving readers a Christian counterpart," she says. "Was it possible to write page-turning suspense with a spiritual message that could impact lives?" Terri started working on some ideas that were already forming in her mind.

Before she could submit her ideas to a publisher, she needed to find an agent who knew the Christian market. "I wanted someone who loved the Lord and who would set the ministry of my writing as a higher priority than the money," she says. She had found one agent, but on the day she was to sign the contract with him, she felt uneasy. Her husband, Ken, prayed with her, asking God to let her know if she was not supposed to sign that contract and to send the right agent so she could get on with what she felt called to do.

Two hours later, Ken was driving in his car, listening to Christian radio again. He heard Greg Johnson talking about a book he had coauthored—and also noted that Greg was a Christian literary agent. Remembering his prayer of that morning, he pulled over to a pay phone and tracked down Greg in Colorado Springs. He told Greg about Terri, and Greg said he would talk to her. Then Ken called Terri.

Though uncertain, Terri called Greg. "The moment Greg and I began talking, I knew that this was the agent God had sent to answer our prayers," Terri says. "Peace fell over me, and I could see that he was excited about my books."

Greg was able to quickly sell Terri's four-book suspense series to Zondervan. Now Terri had one more decision to make: Should she call herself Terri Herrington, her name before she met Ken and the name her readers were used to, or use her new name, Terri Blackstock?

Again Terri had to wrestle with ambition—the potential of bringing her former readers over to her new books—and integrity. This time integrity and faith won out. "I was worried that if I wrote under my former name, readers would read one of my Christian novels, then go back and find an earlier steamy romance, and get confused. I didn't want anyone thinking I was writing both things at the same time." She had made the break, and she wanted her Christian testimony to be clear.

Now Terri continues to write books that reflect her passion to help Christians grow spiritually. "I think my calling is to challenge Christians," she says. "I was such a sleeping Christian for so many years, I want to wake others up and inspire them to bear fruit."

Sometimes the old temptations to focus on money or the best-seller list rear up to distract her. "A few years ago, we had money problems," she says. "My husband said it was okay if we had to sell our cars and our house. When we were trying to sell the house, I was consumed with money. It was tempting to say, 'If I could just do two more books, we'd be set.' " But then she would be encroaching on what she knows is her higher calling—being a mother to her three children. Although they are older, she knows the idea that they don't need her anymore is not from God. She tries not to write when they are awake and at home. When she breaks this rule to meet a deadline, she suffers. Long hours at the computer have led to back problems. "God still teaches me hard lessons," she says.

Terri says her favorite line in Jesus' parable of the Prodigal Son is, "But while he was still a long way off, his father saw him and was filled with compassion for him. . . ." (Luke 15:20b). It reminds her so much of her own story. "I wish my story were different," she says. "I wish I could say that the Lord told me as a young girl that I was supposed to be a writer and that I'd use my gift for him from the beginning. There's no telling what he might have done with me. But what I can say is that the Lord took what I gave him, when I gave it to him, and made all the ugliness beautiful. He's turned all of my past sins into a testimony for him."

Terri says that there was a time, through all of her wandering, when her best hope was that she would stop grieving God. "I didn't think he would ever be able to use me again," she says. "And God said, 'Watch me.' "

"Whether I write for unbelievers or believers, it always ends up being about God's love, one way or another, because it's all inspired by his love."

ATHOL DICKSON is an architect by trade, but in his midthirties he started writing a novel. His first book, *Whom Shall I Fear?* was published in 1996, followed by *Every Hidden Thing* and *They Shall See God.* His books have received glowing reviews from sources such as *The New York Times Sunday Magazine, Library Journal, The Fort Worth Star Telegram, The Dallas Morning News,* and *Booklist,* among others. He has also finished a nonfiction book of Christian theology based on his years of studying the Torah, entitled *The Gospel According to Moses.* His journey to publication was, like his mystery novels, full of unexpected twists and turns.

The Test

A thol Dickson says there's no reason for him to be a writer. He didn't study it. He didn't grow up with a passion for it. He didn't even consider it until he was in his midthirties. Yet he believes that God has given him a gift, which he calls "typing in tongues." Like any other spiritual gift, it is to be used to build up the body of Christ and point people to God's love. "I believe God has given me this gift for the same reason he gives everything," Athol says, "so I can love him with all my heart and love my neighbor as myself. I do that by writing about his love, about the various ways we cut ourselves off from his love, and about the one who is the way back to his love."

It is a gift that came, in some ways, through the back door. And it has been tested by fire.

Though Athol did not consider writing as a child, he did learn early on what it feels like to, as he puts it, "live in the creative rush." As a little boy he loved to draw, and he spent hours sketching things. "Even then," he says, "I think I felt a connection between the creative act and the Creator. Unbelievers call that feeling a 'creative rush,' but I know what it is. It is being in touch for a moment with what it means to be made in God's image. I have wanted to live within that creative rush ever since I can remember."

Athol's father was the son of a sharecropper who was a Seventh-day Adventist, and his mother was the daughter of a state judge in Oklahoma. He grew up in Dallas, Texas. When he was eleven, he rose to his feet at the end of a fire-and-brimstone revival sermon and "walked the aisle." Soon thereafter he was baptized by a man named Brother Cloud, who wore horn-rimmed glasses and hip waders. His parents gave him a King James Bible, and for the next five years Athol was passionate about the Lord. At age sixteen, he entered the fringes of the "Jesus movement" and got a new Bible with a tie-dyed cover.

Then Athol met his first girlfriend, and suddenly Jesus didn't seem so important. "We were crazy about each other, right up to the day she broke my heart," he says. "It felt like God had abandoned me." Athol took to smoking marijuana to ease the pain. "This led to other drugs, just like everyone said it would," he says. Four years later, he was an amphetamine addict.

With the help of his family, he left Dallas for a while and kicked the speed habit, but he never really resolved other problems. He entered college and married "for all the wrong reasons." He filled the empty place his addiction had left behind with binge drinking. When drunk, he abused his wife. She divorced him.

Athol moved into a one-room apartment without mirrors. For a year, he spent as much time as possible in that apartment, alone, away from other people, "for fear the animal would come out of me again," he says.

"I faced the fact that I was lost, but had no idea what to do about it. I quit getting drunk so often. I read a book on Zen Buddhism. It seemed to make sense, so I became a Buddhist congregation of one, sitting cross-legged among candles in my little room, chanting, meditating, trying to purge my self from me. It didn't work. I was still me, still lost, still afraid of mirrors. Desperate, I opened my old Bible—not the tie-dyed one, the one my parents gave me on the day I was baptized. And right then and there, Jesus took me back in spite of everything."

Athol went back to school to study art, specializing in architecture. But the harsh reality that art does not pay became clear as his older friends began graduating and taking menial jobs to support their "creative habit." Athol wanted to live comfortably, so he changed universities and changed his major to architecture.

He graduated, then remarried. After a three-year internship and a three-day examination, he became a registered architect. He started a small firm, working out of his spare bedroom. After a dozen years or so, Athol was fairly successful financially but found himself spending far more time tending to his business—which had grown to fifteen employees—than being creative. "More than a decade after I entered college with the hope of living a creative life, I was no closer to my goal," he says.

Athol felt miserable. He prayed for guidance. The idea came to him that he could do something creative in his spare time. Since he loved to read, he decided to try writing. One weekend he began with a few words written longhand on a note pad. It took him two years to finish that first book. It was a murder mystery, with a vaguely sketched subplot about a man who learns to lean on God when the chips are down. He let a few close friends and family read it, then put it in a box and tried to forget about it. He had heard the stories about how difficult it is to get published.

Then he met a man who was an editor at the *Dallas Morning News*. In their very first conversation they discussed writing, and Athol told him about his book. The man offered to read it. Athol gave it to him—and waited. After almost three months of silence, he had pretty much decided that the book was a stinker and the editor was too embarrassed to tell him so. "Actually, I figured maybe he was put off by the Christian theme of the book, since he didn't strike me as a particularly religious man. All along as I wrote the book, I had tried to keep from being preachy, but I didn't know if I had succeeded. Apparently not."

But without warning, the editor called Athol to set up a meeting. When they got together, one of the first things the man said was, "Athol, I think you're about to commit literature with this thing." He followed that up by slapping eight single-spaced typewritten pages of notes on the table. "At that point, I knew the book must be pretty good, otherwise why would he waste so much time on it? And the very serious suggestion he made was to put *more* emphasis on the spiritual subtheme of the book!"

Athol took most of the editor's advice, including the part about strengthening the Christian theme. The editor talked up Athol's book to another editor friend of his who had won three Pulitzer

Prizes. That fellow wanted to read it, and when he was done, he offered to send it to his agent in New York.

"I was delighted, of course," Athol says. "But then I learned that his agent was a Jewish woman, and I got nervous. After rewriting the novel with my new editor friend's ideas in mind, the context of Christianity was front and center. Would a Jewish woman want to have anything to do with it?"

It took her about a month to respond. Athol was on pins and needles the whole time. When she called, she said, "I love this book. I think it needs to be published. I'd like to represent you. The only thing is" (*Here it comes,* Athol thought), "I think you should accentuate the spiritual subtheme a bit more."

More? Athol was shocked. "For the first time, I really believed that God must have a hand in all of this. Other people write thousands of pages and spend years honing their craft, weathering dozens, even hundreds of rejections before getting a New York agent to represent them. This was the first fiction I had written since a creative writing course in college, and I hadn't made any effort to find an agent, yet here she was, an owner of one of New York's most successful agencies, taking me on. Even more wonderful was the fact that this Jewish woman was telling me to be overt about my faith in my fiction! I thought surely God must want me to write."

Within two weeks, the agent got Simon and Schuster interested. An acquisitions editor had contacted her, hinting at a multiple book contract. The agent called Athol, and he sensed an excitement in her voice, as if this was much easier than usual, and perhaps the editor's interest a bit stronger than usual. There was just the one proviso: the editor wanted Athol to make the religious aspect of the novel more "generic."

"What does that mean?" Athol asked.

The agent said, "Oh, I don't think it's serious. Maybe if you just replace the word *Jesus* with the word *God.*"

"I wish I could say I wasn't even tempted," Athol says. "But I tried to tell myself God must want this, since he brought me this far through no effort of my own. My wife and I prayed about it for two weeks. But then I turned down the offer."

Athol had a big-time New York agent and a big-time New York publisher sending him letters and calling on the phone. He imagined a dazzling career, filled with readings and book signings and whatever else it was big-time authors do. And best of all, it was obviously all God's will. "Then, poof! It vanished," Athol says. The agent did not understand his decision, of course. She was very curt to him the last time they spoke. Simon and Schuster gave the manuscript all of thirty seconds' consideration before moving on to the next one in their infinite supply. And Athol was back to being an architect with a writing hobby.

Athol did not understand any of it. What was God doing? Many friends, including Christian friends, told him he had made a terrible mistake. He began to question his decision. Maybe he had misunderstood what God wanted. "Maybe I was supposed to tone down the Jesus stuff a little, just to get my foot in, and then take advantage of my bully pulpit later, after God made me a fabulously successful author with pals like Stephen King and John Grisham," Athol says.

He had told his story to a family friend, whose pastor had suggested he get a second opinion on the manuscript from a literary agency specializing in Christian authors. He sent the agency the manuscript, and within a few weeks, Athol signed a contract with Zondervan Publishing House. That novel, *Whom Shall I Fear?*, is still in print, but never became the bestseller Athol had envisioned. It made him wonder if he should have compromised with Simon and Schuster.

Then about a year after the book hit the shelves, Athol went to a book signing in his hometown. Such events are not usually well attended, and this one had an especially small turnout with only half a dozen people showing up. He felt embarrassed by the meager turnout. But the last woman in line said she found the book impossible to put down.

"Well, thanks," Athol said. "I tried to make it a real page-turner."

"No," she said. "That's not what I mean. I mean I *couldn't* stop reading. I stayed up until three-thirty in the morning, all alone in my apartment, reading and reading, and when I was done, I thought, 'If that's what it's like to have Jesus in your life, I want him,' and I called a friend of mine, a Christian girl, and she told me what to pray, and I let Jesus in my heart, right then and there."

Athol says, "By then I was crying and the lady was crying, and ever since, I haven't doubted for a minute that I did the right thing by leaving Jesus in my book."

Athol has continued to keep Jesus in his books. He sometimes writes with Christians in mind, hoping his stories will help them see how they can get out of the way and let the Lord's love flow more freely into the world. One way or another, he says, "it always ends up being about God's love, because it's all inspired by his love for me. Some people don't get the love in my books. They say the books are too rough around the edges. I guess that's probably true. But I write from a heart that holds a lot of scars (left over from those days of darkness), and I think that's what touches those few who read the words and sense the Spirit in them."

Worldly success will not necessarily follow just because we are in the center of God's will, fulfilling our calling. Everything seemed to fall into place for Athol, and God's blessing seemed to be fueling the events, yet at the heart of it, he was being asked to deny his Lord. He could have compromised, but he didn't. Perhaps he would have sold a lot more books had he stayed with a New York publisher and taken out the word *Jesus*. But then, would he have gained the whole world but lost the one thing that mattered—the only thing that has the power to change a person's life?

Writing is Athol's gift, but it's given, as all gifts are, with some strings attached. He has to work hard at cultivating it, and he has to use it in the right way: to express the love of God to a loveless world.

Each of us has our own way of fulfilling that very same purpose. Each of us is responsible for recognizing and cultivating our gift and keeping our motives pure. Each of us faces the temptation, sooner or later, to compromise just a little, to rationalize and perhaps even convince ourselves that the compromise is opportunity, rather than what it is—a turning from the path of life.

After all, as Athol says, "Near as I can tell, God only gave one gift with no strings attached."

CHAPTER 8

God's Stretching Places

"Any experience, when offered up to God,

can become your gateway to joy."

— ELISABETH ELLIOT

"I will cling to the Lord Christ as the burr to the cloth."

—KATHERINE LUTHER

FRANCINE RIVERS

"I've made a conscious decision to give the gifts Jesus gave me back to him in gratitude and in service. It's my prayer that whatever stories I write now or in the future will be used to his good purpose in bringing others to head and heart knowledge of him."

FRANCINE RIVERS published a number of novels in the general romance market until 1993, when she released her first book in the Christian book market with Tyndale House Publishers. *A Voice in the Wind* has sold nearly 300,000 copies, and her subsequent books have all sold very well. Her book *The Atonement Child,* released in the spring of 1997, was the number one bestselling hardcover fiction title in the Christian bookstore market for four months. *Redeeming Love, The Last Sin Eater, Leota's Garden,* and the five novellas in her LINEAGE OF GRACE series have also appeared on the bestseller list. Francine was named to the Hall of Fame by the Romance Writers of America in 1997. She has won awards for her books that range from Golden Medallions to Silver Pens.

What God Took Away

Ever since she was a child, Francine Rivers knew she would someday be a writer. "I felt the calling, even though it wasn't until I became a born-again Christian that I came to understand that writing is a means of worshiping the Lord," she says. She studied English and journalism in college but, like many of us, put the call on hold while she married and had children.

When Francine's three children were young, she was an avid reader of romance novels. In fact, she admits she was addicted. Once she said to her husband, Rick, "I could do better than this." He said, "Go for it." She did. Once she started writing in earnest, Rick encouraged her to try writing full time. Francine gave herself five years to be "financially successful."

She was. She published thirteen novels, won awards for her books, and was twice voted by readers as one of the top ten romance writers in America. She made "very good money" and measured her success in terms of advances, print runs, and books sold. "I got to the point where success was all I cared about," Francine says.

Although Francine was raised by Christian parents and attended church most of her life, she says she didn't realize she needed a Master as well as a Savior. "I thought I was a Christian," she says, "but I was not born again. Nor did I understand what God's love really is. I was master of my life. I wanted control."

But the success Francine found did not fulfill her. Restless for change, Rick and Francine and their children decided to start anew: Rick would start his own business, and they would move closer to family. As they were unpacking the moving van, a neighbor boy came up to them and asked, "Are you Jewish?"

"No," they said, "why?"

"Then have I got a church for you!" the boy said. Francine and then Rick and the children started attending and discovered that there was indeed something special about this church. People were serious about living their faith. That is when Francine and each member of her family learned what it means to allow God to take control. Quite simply, "I became born again, and God changed my life."

But then something frightening happened. Francine could no longer write. She recalls, "For almost four years I couldn't write anymore. It was like God just shut it off. I could not write anything that made any sense at all. It was a strange experience to say, 'Lord, you take control of my life,' and then wham! that door—writing—is closed." Looking back, Francine believes God took away her vocation for a time because writing had become the focus of her life—her escape and her idol.

It was time to refocus on Christ and his Word and get her priorities rearranged. She asked God to replace her avid interest in romance novels with a hunger for his Word. He answered that prayer: She read the entire Bible five times in three years.

She and Rick also hosted a Bible study in their home. One day as the group was studying the book of Hosea, something in Francine suddenly clicked. This was the story the Lord wanted her to write! She was to put the Hosea story into a different time period and illustrate the kind of love that would make a prostitute change her ways.

Francine wrote *Redeeming Love* (first released by Bantam in 1991, then rereleased by Multnomah in 1997). "It was a wonderful experience to write that book. I felt as if the Lord was right by my side the whole time I wrote." God gave her back the gift of writing.

But Francine says she doesn't even look at the bestseller list now. "It just takes your focus off what you're supposed to focus on: doing the Lord's work, whatever it is." Now, she says, she measures her success as a writer not in terms of dollars and print runs, but in terms of whether she is following God and using her talents to serve him. "I trust he will take whatever I do and use it for his purposes."

Any gift can become an idol if we value the gift more than the Giver. Francine muses, "It was when the writing no longer mattered to me, at the place where all that mattered was following the Lord, that the door [to writing] opened again. The gift was not the fact that now I was writing again, but that God took first place in my life. God was saying, 'Now that you have your priorities straight and I'm number one in your life, I will give you back what I gave you in the first place.'"

When God takes something away, it is to give back something greater. The gift is always a gateway to the Giver, not the end itself. Francine's experience taught her that she needs to "choose things that enlighten, encourage, and assist me in my walk with Christ. And I need to remember that even too much of a good thing can be bad. When I'm open to the Holy Spirit, he tells me when I cross that line. We need to allow God to soften our hearts to the point where we are sensitive to what the Holy Spirit tells us—then obey what he says."

Obedience in terms of her career means writing books that illuminate what it means to be a Christian—and staying grounded in the Word. Writing is a means of learning more about the Lord for Francine. "It's a way of searching myself, uncovering faults and weaknesses, and searching the Scripture for solutions. I use writing now to answer questions I have in my own walk with the Lord."

As an example, she points to the main character, Hadassah, in *A Voice in the Wind*. "Because I long for the kind of faith the early Christians had, I created a character who is too frightened to share her faith with others, but who eventually has the courage to face the lions rather than recant. She also learns to forgive those who sought her death. Hadassah is the kind of Christian I want to be." Writing about Hadassah made Francine face her own deficiencies and underscored the need to allow Christ absolute sovereignty in all areas of her life. "Without Jesus I can do nothing. With him all things are possible. I learned these things in a new way when I wrote the MARK OF THE LION books."

Francine felt the call to write, but God let her do it her own way for a while. Then, when she came to him with the gift in hand, he took it away for a time. As she left the gift on the altar and drew near to the Giver, God changed her. Then he gave her back her gift, knowing that she was ready to use it for his purposes. Francine's greatest hope is that her books "will encourage other Christians who have the same struggles I have, and that the books can be used as tools in presenting the Gospel to unsaved friends and family members. There are so many people who would rather die than pick up a Bible. Fiction can serve in a nonthreatening way to open minds and, I hope, hearts to the Word of God." Letters from readers attest that God is fulfilling this hope.

Where is your gift? In your own hands, on the altar, or in the hands of the Giver? Like the little boy's lunch offered up to Jesus, sometimes God takes our loaf and breaks it. But broken and in the hands of Jesus, those pieces can feed thousands, whereas unbroken the loaf could only feed a small boy.

"My intention is to share the love of God with my readers. I want people simply to know that God loves them. Sometimes even when you know God, you can feel that he's forgotten you. But that's never true; it's God's very nature to love us. I want people to experience some of that love in my work."

JAN KARON is the author of the wildly popular MITFORD series books, centering on a fictional small town in North Carolina. She won the 1996 American Booksellers Book of the Year for *At Home in Mitford,* and the Christy Award in 2000 for *A New Song.* Each of her books now becomes a bestseller, but it wasn't always that way. In fact, the road to success as an author for Jan Karon has been uphill most of the way. Here she shares the journey of her call to "write books for God" and what it means for any of us to find and use our gift, not just our talent, to fulfill our calling.

Through the Fire

Jan Karon wanted to be a writer since she was ten. She remembers playing the card game called Author, with pictures of authors such as Henry Longfellow, Henry David Thoreau, Jane Austen, and Charles Dickens. She was an omnivorous reader, and a desire began to grow in her. "I wanted to be able to give to others some of the joy and adventure and excitement that was given to me so freely when I read a book."

But Jan had no idea how to turn her desire into reality. She went into advertising "sort of accidentally," and found she was very good at it. She won many awards and made a good living at it. But something was happening to her soul. By the time she was forty-two years old, she felt completely empty inside. "I was so starved for God," Jan says, "that it was more than I could bear. One night I got on my knees on my bed, and I begged God to save my soul. I asked Jesus to come into my heart."

Though she knew she needed Jesus, it was not an easy conversion. "What I was asking for frightened me, because I felt God would reach down—being the policeman he was—and snatch me up by the scruff of the neck and give me what-for. Well, he did—I needed what-for—but in his own wonderful way. Then my life began to change dramatically."

Jan became very hungry for the Word of God and eventually found a church home where she learned to study the Bible, pray, and lean on God. In the process, the old prompting to write books grew stronger. Jan spent two years in very focused prayer about what she began to realize was a gift. She asked God to show her how to become a writer and asked him to either open the door very wide or slam it in her face if this wasn't his will.

After the two years of prayer, the door did begin to open, and she had a peace in her heart that she was supposed to walk through that door. She quit her job in advertising and headed for the mountains. She bought a small cottage near some family members, bought a used computer, and began writing.

Though she had the peace and conviction that this was what she was supposed to do, her new chosen path was strewn with rocks and ruts. "I sat down to write what I thought would be a pretty good book, and found it was not good at all," Jan says. "The characters were flat and very one-dimensional, and I didn't know where the story was going. I began to say, 'Why am I doing this?' "

She had sacrificed much to follow her dream. Her income was cut in half; for a year she didn't even own a car. Was it all for naught? Was her dream turning into a nightmare? All her fears surfaced: of being a laughingstock, letting down the people who had prayed so hard for her, letting herself down, letting God down.

It was a time of testing, a time of hammering, a time of shaping. "God wanted to put me through the fire like clay to make me into some usable vessel," she says now. "By usable I mean simply someone who could write a book." For reasons of his own, it seems that God often keeps us from realizing our dream until we have gone through some time of testing, molding, shaping, and suffering. "Maybe some people can write books or do things for God without being tested, but I can't imagine how that could happen," Jan says.

When Jan Karon went off to the mountains to write books, she did not realize at the time that she was to write books for God. She knew she wanted to get out of advertising, she knew she had a talent and the desire to write, and she believed that God had made a path for her to do so. But at some point in that time of despair, she turned it all over to God.

That's when her talent became a gift, a vocation, a calling. Jan explains the difference: "A talent is a bold running creek. A gift is an ocean. Unfathomable, it goes very, very far down to the ocean floor. A gift is a bigger thing—you can draw on it more deeply." A gift is a talent that has been given back to God to transform into an ocean. From that ocean, the gifted person can draw again and again, for there is no end to the Source.

God gives us the talent, but it's up to us what we do with it. If we turn it over to him, it can become a gift. If we don't do anything with it, we will suffer in some way, Jan believes. Not that God will punish us. But if we don't use our talents and let them become gifts, we—and the world—will be diminished in some way.

But if we don't hold back, if we recognize the gift and turn it back to God, then what we thought might be a vocation or even avocation becomes a calling. "It's not a calling as long as you're keeping it to yourself," Jan says. A calling is a vocation that has been turned over to God to use as he will. "Things really began to happen in a much deeper way when I turned my work, all of it, over to God."

One night during that time of prayer and near despair, Jan was lying in bed when a vision of a priest walking down a village street arose in her mind's eye. "I decided to submit it to my imagination and see where it went," she says. "And then it went to a dog named Barnabas and a boy named Doolie, and the story began to tell itself to me."

Jan worked on the first book in the Mitford series, and it was published serially in her local newspaper, *The Blowing Rocket*. "The newspaper sold for ten cents a copy, and my payment was a copy of the newspaper!"

The road to publication and eventually fame was uphill all the way. She put the manuscript into the hands of an agent, who sat on it for a year and a half. She took it out of the agent's hands and began to circulate it herself. It was rejected again and again. Somehow her faith in this work remained intact; by this time she was sure of her calling. "I continued to believe there was at least a small audience for this kind of idiosyncratic book," Jan says. "Even though nobody murdered anyone or raped anybody or even used a cuss word, there had to be somebody like me who would like to read a book that based itself upon delightful characters and people with good hearts."

Eventually a publisher bought it but did little to distribute it. Jan took it upon herself to do whatever she could to promote the book. Though she could not afford the expensive trade journal *Publisher's Weekly,* she subscribed anyway and studied each issue, giving herself a crash course in every aspect of bookselling. She contacted booksellers personally, went to book signings, did whatever it took to get the word out about this book she believed in. Eventually, one bookseller was so enamored with the two Mitford books that were by then in print, that he suggested she talk to a famous New York City agent. Jan thought there was no way a powerful New York agent would ever get on the same wavelength with her, but it turned out the agent did understand and liked the books. She took them to Penguin, who also really got behind the books. The rest is history, with more than eight million copies of the Mitford books sold.

Reflecting on the success of the Mitford books, Jan acknowledges that it's not something she could ever have brought about herself. "My verse for this whole part of my life is based on John 15:16: 'You did not choose me, [Jan,] but I chose you and appointed you to go and bear fruit—fruit that will last.' "

The fruit of Jan's ministry is seen in the letters she receives from readers or the people who come up to her and clasp her hand and look deep into her eyes and say, "I cannot tell you how God has used your books in my life." Though Jan knows she has answered the call on her life to "write books for God—period," God is in charge of the harvest. "Although it's a calling, I don't pretend to think that I know how to write books that will affect people in this deep way. These are God's books, this is his work, his ministry. He simply gives me the stamina, the imagination, the time, whatever it takes to bring them into being in the real world."

Jan believes we all have talents that can become anointed gifts. All are called to the task of bearing fruit that will remain. Why do people not always respond? "I think that everyone knows the fear of using their gifts, though they may never articulate it," Jan says. "In that deep well, in that place where they know God is—no matter how atheistic they may be, there's God in them somewhere struggling to be known and expressed—deep down in that place they're scared to death to exercise their gifts, because they know there will be sacrifice. There *will* be sacrifice. I don't care where you are, I don't care how much money you have to tide you over while you're trying to write your book or change careers or whatever, God is going to call us all into a hard place to work for him. God can't give you a gift to touch other people in a variety of ways unless he has put you in the valley in a variety of ways. That's the only way we can ever reach people."

The challenge is before you. Discover your gift, ask God to anoint it, and be prepared to go through the fire. Will you accept the challenge? If you do, cling to the words of John 15:16 that Jan spoke of, and also Isaiah 43:2: "When you pass through the waters, I will be with you; and when you pass through the rivers, they will not sweep over you. When you walk through the fire, you will not be burned; the flames will not set you ablaze." They will only refine you into a vessel that is both beautiful and useful, a container for the living water of God's grace to the world.

JANE KIRKPATRICK

"There is something in the word, and paying attention to the word, that is healing. Story has a way of connecting us; we find ourselves within the story, and in the finding there is healing."

JANE KIRKPATRICK is an author, speaker, and mental health consultant who works with Native American and non-Indian communities. She is the author of award-winning essays, articles, and humor that have appeared in more than fifty publications, including *Country, Old House Journal, Decision, In-Fisherman,* and *Daily Guideposts.* She has also published *Homestead,* the story of how she and her husband left suburbia and moved to a remote part of Oregon to tame the wilderness. Her first novel, *A Sweetness to the Soul,* was awarded the prestigious Wrangler Award as the Outstanding Western Novel of 1995 from the National Cowboy Hall of Fame and Western Heritage Center. That book was the first in a four-book series, which also included *Love to Water My Soul, A Gathering of Finches,* and *Mystic Sweet Communion.* Her next series is called THE KINSHIP & COURAGE SERIES.

Into the Wilderness and Beyond

Jane Kirkpatrick has a phrase that sums up her understanding of her calling: "The right word at the right time to offer solace and encouragement to people." It's based on Proverbs 25:11: "A word aptly spoken is like apples of gold in settings of silver." All that Jane does revolves around the idea of the apt word, spoken (or written) in God's time, in God's way. From that comes healing.

Of course, it took years for this to come into focus for Jane. As a young person, she wrote all the time—"dreadful little poems" as a child, essays in high school. One essay, "What Jesus Means to Me," won a contest. Jane began to consider writing as a career. In college, she felt torn between writing and counseling. She had a deep desire to help heal people. One influential professor talked her into pursuing communications. Jane did some public relations writing and public speaking and enjoyed that. Then another professor who was working with adolescents referred by the court asked her to work with a parents group to increase their success with their challenging children. The experience changed her life—Jane got her master's degree in social work. She moved to Oregon, worked with families with children who had disabilities, and eventually became the director of the mental health center in Deschutes County. She found her work very fulfilling.

In 1976 Jane married Jerry, a man sixteen years older than she who had a dream: to buy some land and tame it. In June 1979, when they bought what the locals called "Starvation Point"—160 acres of "rattlesnake and rock" along the John Day River in a remote part of Oregon—Jane felt secretly terrified. "I enjoyed *reading* diaries of homesteaders, admiring their stamina and grit; but I knew I didn't want to endure the same kinds of hardships myself," she says.

For five years she fought the idea of actually living on Starvation Point, of going into the wilderness and doing all the backbreaking work of homesteading that land. It was Jerry's dream, not hers. The idea of starting from scratch—with no piped water, electricity, or any other modern conveniences anywhere near the property, not to mention people—seemed totally unrealistic to Jane. "I have no desire to live in the wilderness," she told Jerry.

"I have enough desire for both of us," Jerry answered.

"But if I go just for you, then when things go wrong, I'll blame you," Jane told him. She had to find a way to trust the dream for herself.

And so the dream—Jerry's dream—shimmered on the horizon.

One day, at a church retreat on finding God's will, Jane knew that God wanted her and Jerry to do this thing—to build a homestead at Starvation Point. It was very clear: God was asking her to trust him.

This was not an easy task for someone who calls herself a control addict. ("I'm in recovery now," she says.) At the time, she knew God was asking her to let him work in her life in a new way. The one thing she knew for sure was that he had promised not to abandon her. That was what she clung to.

Nevertheless, she struggled to make sense of it. God was asking her to leave a job she loved and—do what? Jerry would do the bulk of the work of homesteading. She'd help, of course. "But what," she asked God, "am *I* to do there?"

A word came to her: "Write."

Jane says, "I remember thinking, *That's interesting.*" She recalled how much she'd always enjoyed writing. So she stepped into her own wilderness by first taking some writing courses at the community college. She began to sell her articles. She took that as confirmation. Another confirmation came when *Private Pilot* published her first big spread, and it came out on Jane's last day of work at the clinic. "What it gave me was a sense that whatever we would face in the days ahead, we would not be alone," she says.

She'd need that certainty to face the difficulties of harnessing a spring for drinking water; securing electricity; building a barn without the help of electrical power; living in a home so far from supplies; laying miles of phone wire—twice—in 110-degree heat; losing acres of crops to wind and days of work to floods; and finally, experiencing the terror and agony of a plane crash.

Difficult as these challenges were, what loomed even larger, Jane says, were the emotional obstacles, the barriers of the mind: guilt, fear, a sense of unworthiness. These were the biggest threats to success. They are the obstacles any of us face when we're called into any kind of wilderness, Jane realized. She and Jerry could not have foreseen many of the difficulties—physical, mental, or emotional—when they made the decision to move into the wilderness. But neither could they know of the miracles, large and small, and the people they would come to know and care about, who would help them, heal them, bring humor to their lives, share their tears and laughter, and take them closer to each other—and to God.

When they finally got electricity to the homestead, Jane began to write to her friends about their experiences. Several wrote back, telling her how they savored her letters, reading them aloud as if they were chapters in a book.

That sparked an idea for Jane. Why not try to put all they'd experienced and learned into a book? While very few people actually do what they had done—headed off into the wilderness and made a life there—plenty of people ended up in "wilderness experiences" of one kind or another. Divorce, abandonment, illness, death of a loved one, and financial failure all can bring the same sort of mental and emotional challenges Jane and Jerry faced while trying to tame the wilderness.

So the book *Homestead* was born. She sold it on the strength of her seventy-five page proposal and some sample chapters. Jane felt anew that sense of inadequacy. But, she says, again she was reminded that she was not in this venture alone; God had led them to the land, walked with them through the experiences, and was now opening a door to tell others of his faithfulness, even on

Starvation Point. *Homestead* appeared in print the day before her forty-fifth birthday.

In addition to writing *Homestead,* Jane continued to write short articles and essays. One she wrote, about fishing as a mosaic of her marriage, generated letters and calls from men who were deeply moved by the essay. One man wrote, "You have described the relationship I had with my wife before she died; reading it was like reading a tribute to her."

"It was the first time I gathered I might be able to write something that would heal people," Jane says. "Up until then I had been writing features and funny stories. Now I saw that my words could create an emotional connection, as well." She recalled some writer saying that "if you can write essays that can touch people, you can write fiction."

Could writing fiction be the next adventure for Jane? A lover of history, she had read about another Jane, Jane Herbert, born in 1848, whose life paralleled hers in several ways. She, too, had wanted to build a homestead; she, too, married a man sixteen years older than herself who was a dreamer. All the while Jane and Jerry built their homestead, Jane Kirkpatrick mulled over Jane Herbert's life along another remote Oregon river, with Native Americans as neighbors. Why had she never had children, though she seemed to love them so? Could it be because as a young girl, three of Jane Herbert's siblings had died of diphtheria within days of each other? "What a great story that would be to tell," Jane remarked to Jerry. "But a real writer should do that, or a historian, or at least someone who has lived in this county for years."

"You should write it," he replied. "That story is talking to you."

But, Jane wondered, would anyone else be as interested in it as she was?

"Just write it," Jerry said, "and if people don't like it, they can write their own version."

Jane didn't know then that the story had something to tell her as she wrote it. So Jane decided yes, she would write Jane Herbert's story. The very next day, when she went to a historical society meeting, a man asked her what she did. Jane replied, "I'm a writer."

The man asked her what she was writing. She told him about Jane Herbert. He said, "You should meet my cousin—she owns Jane Herbert's original property."

So Jane embarked on a new adventure—writing historical fiction. Again she didn't know for sure if she could do it. All she had was her commitment and the faith that she would not be in this alone. She wrote between four and eight in the morning—the only time she had to write when she wasn't helping raise watermelons, haying, and assisting with their small herd of cattle. "I'd give myself until five o'clock to 'assume the position' of a writer," she says. "I tried to talk myself out of it umpteen times. Then I'd remind myself my commitment was not to write the Great American Novel, but to just write this story and trust I was not alone in the telling. By five o'clock, I always found I had something to write."

Jane found herself an agent, and the story was sold right away. *A Sweetness to the Soul* came out in 1995. When Jane received the advance money, she wrote a check for her tithe on it but didn't mail it before she went to speak at a Christian businessmen's gathering. After she spoke, she stayed and listened to the next presenter. The man spoke from the book of Haggai, about testing the Lord, about how when we tithe, God is faithful in providing for *all* our needs. What Jane needed, then, was not more money, but rather confirmation that other people thought her writing was worthwhile. If someone other than my friends and family would acknowledge the value of the story, she thought, then she'd know God was still confirming this writing direction. So instead of claiming the abundance of financial reward, she claimed acknowledgment of the ministry. When she got home, she wrote *award* in the memo section of her tithe check and sent it off.

Four months later, she received in the mail a letter from the Western Heritage Center, saying that *A Sweetness to the Soul* was awarded the Wrangler Award of the National Cowboy Hall of Fame and was named Western Heritage Center's Outstanding Western Novel of 1995. "I was in shock," Jane says. No wonder: Others who have been awarded Wranglers include Louis L'Amour, Sydney Pollack, James Michener, John Wayne, James Stewart, Jack Palance, Clint Eastwood, Kevin Costner, Jon Voight, Gene Hackman, and Robert Duvall. And now—Jane Kirkpatrick!

"I felt so amazed at the graciousness of God—it was one of those incredible moments," Jane recalls. "And what made it even better was that I got the letter as we were on the way to church, so I was able to share it with our faith community."

Jane can tell about other times when she committed something to God and he worked in amazing ways. Her books always seem to be inspired by some bit of historical fact that raises questions in her mind, questions that won't let her go. When writing *A Gathering of Finches*, the story of Cassie Hendrick Stearns Simpson, she needed more information. She knew that Cassie's husband had given her five acres of a garden, what is now Shore Acres State Park, as a gift. But in all her research, she found lots of information about the husband yet little about Cassie. What kind of woman would inspire a man to give her such a gift? And why did so little information exist on her?

These questions spurred her on, but all she could find were vague remembrances of family members including a story that had something to do with the water system of a frontier town. Jane called that city and was given the name of a retired historian who helped her research. But still, no dates of births or marriages emerged.

But one day, Jane's elderly researcher called to say that at a Salvation Army board meeting he sat next to a man who turned out to be none other than the great-nephew of Cassie Simpson—and he had Cassie's family Bible, which contained the missing link Jane had been looking for! "What but divine intervention could have engineered that?" Jane asks in wonder. She interviewed the man and had to totally rewrite sections of the book to fit the facts—what she thought had been a romance was actually a tragedy. But she knew it was the story she was supposed to write.

Another time it was not a story puzzle she needed but money—

a part-time job, in fact. But where does one find a part-time job in the middle of the wilderness twenty-five miles from the nearest small town? It was laughable, really. But there it was—that was her need. And the very day she realized the need, she received a letter from a man at the Indian reservation two hours from Jane's land. They needed a social worker.

Jane just couldn't believe what she was reading in that letter. When she left her job to move to the homestead, she thought she was giving up her profession forever. She had always wanted to work with Native Americans, had always felt drawn to them. These things she had told only her husband, no one else. But God, who knew both the deepest desires of her heart and all her practical needs, had engineered events such that a part-time job working with people she'd always been attracted to would become hers. She now works three days a week with children and families, traveling two hours each way to the reservation and staying overnight. Her work there is another way in which she is able to deliver "the right words at the right time" to heal.

Jane looks back on each experience in the wilderness, on each book, on her life now that consists of homesteading, writing, speaking, and working on the reservation—and she marvels at God's hand in her life. "Every time I really did let go and let God take over, what he did was always ten times better than what I could imagine."

Yet letting go is still not easy. "The largest ongoing roadblock I experience is what I call 'the unworthies,' " Jane says. "Who am I to be trying to tell this story; who am I to deprive my husband of all these hours; who am I to think my writing will make any difference? That's when this idea of the commitment is so helpful. I don't have to write the best book but simply tell the story the best way I know how, trusting I am not alone in the telling. Cocreating, as Madeleine L'Engle calls it. When I remember I am a cocreator, I can overcome the unworthies."

Jane likes to share a passage written by the German poet Rainer

Maria Rilke with others who have similar doubts about their effect-iveness. The passage is from *The Book of Hours: Love Poems to God.* Rilke says: "God speaks to us as he makes us, then walks with us silently out of the night. These are the words we dimly hear: You, sent out beyond your recall. Go, to the limits of your longing. Em-body me."

"Maybe longing is another word for the call," Jane muses. "There was this longing in me to heal and to write. If we go out beyond our recall and step out onto the cloud of faith, believing we will not fall through, we are given moments of grace, through which we will, we hope, reveal God to others."

We step out in faith, in commitment, believing God will provide the resources we need to accomplish the task. Just as God provided when he called Jane to go to the wilderness and build a homestead, to write, and to heal through her words. Just as he always provides the way for any one of us to follow, even if he leads us into the wilderness. He always goes ahead, preparing the way, and he never tires of reminding us that we are not alone in the adventure.

ANNE de GRAAF

"I write about what God puts on my heart, stories that grab me and won't let me go. I hope and pray that something in my books will cause both my Christian and non-Christian readers to search further and draw closer to the Lord."

ANNE de GRAAF has written more than eighty children's books and novels. These have sold over four million copies worldwide and have been translated into more than fifty languages. Her novel *Out of the Red Shadow* won the Christy Award 2000 for International Historical Fiction. During the 1999 Frankfurt World Book Fair she was awarded the East-European Christian Literature Award. She is currently working on a series of novels called THE NEGOTIATOR. Born in San Francisco and a graduate of Stanford University, she has lived the past nineteen years in Ireland and the Netherlands with her husband and their two children.

The More Difficult Road

Anne de Graaf knew she wanted to be a writer when she was sixteen. She had won a short story contest in the local newspaper, and the reporter who wrote an article about the contest told her she should think about writing as a career.

In college the classic conflict arose: Should she study something that would pay the bills or something she loved to do? Her mother said to choose something that would enable her to make a living. She became a petroleum engineering major. But a counselor said, "You should do what you want." After much thought, she finally switched to a major in journalism and broadcasting; practical enough (she hoped) to earn a living, yet something that would still give her license to "be nosy" and write.

After college she worked as a reporter in a small town. "It was a good experience, because at a small newspaper you get to do everything," she says. Then she moved from California to Ireland to marry a man she had met two years earlier when she worked in Ireland as an au pair during a year spent studying overseas. They fell in love through their letters, and when Anne returned to Ireland, they were married and lived there a short while after their baby girl was born. Then they moved to the Netherlands so her husband, Erik, could work in the family business, a ship supply company. Soon their little boy was born.

Four years after moving to the Netherlands, Anne had learned enough of the Dutch language to land a job as a journalist at the English desk of the Dutch national press agency. She translated and wrote articles during the night shift, four to eleven. Then she began editing for a Christian publisher, writing children's books, and working as an economics translator for the Dutch government. She eventually left her journalist job to work as a translator for an economic think tank in The Hague.

Always she longed to just write, and finally the day came when she and her husband sat down and figured out that financially she could quit her job and become a full-time writer. "My husband, Erik, has always been so supportive of my writing," Anne says. "I realize how fortunate I am to not have to worry anymore about how we're going to pay the bills. It frees me up to seek the Lord and ask him what he wants me to do."

Though the pressure to depend so much on her income eased up, pressure intensified in other ways. Anne feels a great responsibility to write what she feels God is laying on her heart. Twice a year, in May and November, she takes two weeks to retreat and seek God about her writing. "I walk in the woods with my dogs and pray and write. I ask God what's next, where does he want me to go?"

Inevitably, it seems he asks her to go to difficult places. Writing does not come easily for Anne. "I struggle, I write—it's awful. I seem to have to write a lot of bad stuff before I can do anything good. I throw a lot away and do a lot of rewriting."

Not only is the writing itself hard, but so sometimes is the subject matter. "Sometimes I get a little idea on the retreat, and I start working on it and then the ideas grow. God gives me a passion, I follow it, and I find it's not at all easy." For instance, her HIDDEN HARVEST series began when "the Lord planted a passion in my heart" for Poland. She had been in Poland in 1987 doing research on the Christians living there for a children's book commissioned by a Danish Christian publisher. She says the stories of endurance and persecution she heard then challenged her own faith. For the next five years she drove the fifteen hours back and forth from her home near Rotterdam to Poland several times a year. She interviewed elderly people, researched state archives, and perused old photos while zigzagging through the country looking at the places she was writing about. "The stories would not let me go," she says. She had approached a publisher in England about doing a documentary on the subject. But the Polish Christians did not want her to write their true stories; it was too risky. So she decided to fiction-alize their stories.

Her second adult-novel series, called THE CHILDREN'S VOICES, came to her as a result of her retreat time, as well. "It was another idea that wouldn't let me go," she says. "I was walking when I sensed the Lord saying, 'The children's voices. I'll be there.' I thought about the children of war, and sensed that God wanted me to write about them, give them a voice, describe their plight by means of a thriller."

But she wondered who would publish such an intense story. It was the old tension many writers feel: should they write what pub-lishers want, or write what's on their hearts? Sometimes these two things intersect, and there's no problem. But when a writer's pas-sion does not seem to have an audience, what to do?

Anne plunged ahead, going to a refugee camp in Tanzania to do her research. "It was very difficult in every way," Anne says. The plight of the children and families at the refugee camp broke her heart; she still has nightmares. She returned from the camp physi-cally sick and twenty pounds lighter. She wondered if she had any right at all to be telling the stories of these people. They had abso-lutely nothing, and she was from a privileged background living a comfortable life.

Yet despite the difficulties, she felt that to be obedient, she had to write the book she felt God was laying on her heart. She says sometimes it was like being a blind woman in a dark room, seeking God for the manna of words he faithfully gave, enough for one day only. "My heart was broken sometimes as I wrote this book. I can't distance myself. I don't like the nightmares, the fear and disillusion-ment and despair, but this is all outweighed by an overwhelming sense of hope. The CHILDREN'S VOICES books are based on true stories, interviews, and research with international negotiators. My main character is a woman who finds peace in places of war and hears the children's voices. I've been collecting quotes from chil-dren around the world who have been traumatized by war. And God's own hope is shining through these stories. Despite me. I wish

I could write something easier, but *Into the Nevernight* [the first book in the series] is the book that would not let me go."

In Anne's experience, God rarely leads to the easier road. Not in her writing nor in her life. "I am a Christian who really struggles in her faith," she says. "I don't think it's supposed to be easy. If it's difficult, it's probably from him; then we have to ask for his help. I think it gives God glory when we realize we can't do anything without him. When we look to him, he makes our joy complete; he heals us."

Writing is more like spiritual warfare to Anne than blissful self-expression. First, she has to battle the temptation to get caught up in things other than writing. Two things help here: She keeps strict nine-to-five hours, and she has a chair in her study where she imagines Jesus waits for her to show up for work. "Not that I think everything I write comes from God," she says, "but I do think of my writing as time spent with him."

Prayer is vital, as it is for any task undertaken in God's name. "Prayer is like breathing to me; I choke if I don't get enough of it." She's not trying to sound super spiritual; rather it's a sense of her own inadequacy that drives her to her knees. God calls us to big things, things that seem too hard, and the only way we can do it is to depend totally on him. A friend once told Anne God's strength and leading are like manna; God gives only enough for one day at a time.

"The issue really is obedience," Anne says. "When I obey, then God empowers me to do everything he asks me to do. Then he blesses me and others and my joy is complete." The cycle of blessing starts with obedience, is fueled by prayer and hard work, and ends in joy.

LISA TAWN BERGREN

LISA TAWN BERGREN is the author of ten novels, including *The Bridge,* plus several novellas and two books for children, called *God Gave Us You* and *God Gave Us Two.* In 1998 she received the Lifetime Achievement Award from *Romantic Times.* She also founded the Palisades line of romance books for Questar/Multnomah, and was later an executive editor of fiction for Waterbrook Press, a division of Random House. Lisa lives in Colorado Springs with her husband, Tim, and their two young daughters.

"It is my hope that my books will take readers to a safe place in the world in which they can vicariously experience all that my characters experience, and come away with greater knowledge about how they would like to live their own lives."

Out of the Comfort Zone

Lisa Tawn Bergren might not be a writer today if she hadn't fallen away from her Christian roots for a time. She was raised in the Lutheran church by believing parents. She maintained her faith all through college at the University of California, Irvine, where she majored in English literature. But after college, when she went to Park City, Utah, to "spend a winter as a ski bum," things like prayer and attending church were not high on her priority list. She needed a job, so when a bartending position opened up—that included working Sunday mornings—she took it.

It wasn't long before she realized she was going downhill, and not just on skis. She felt "very lonely, very depressed." Around that time, her mother sent her Frank Peretti's first two books, *This Present Darkness* and *Piercing the Darkness*. She read them in a week. She dug out her old Christian CDs and listened to them. "Through these books and music, God brought me home," Lisa says. "I had this amazing experience in which I saw God; it was as if I caught a glimpse of an inch of his robes, and it floored me. A whole new level of faith entered my life. I left Park City and went straight to Jerusalem. From the den of iniquity to the Holy Land!"

Through her experience, God also gave Lisa direction. "I knew I wanted to be part of the industry that God used to call me home." She did some freelance work with Frontline Music Group, a company that produced alternative Christian music. Through this job, Lisa made contacts within the Christian book publishing industry. She also began writing her first romance novel, and God suddenly opened doors in publishing. The same day she got a job in the marketing department of Questar/Multnomah Publishers, she was also offered a contract for her novel. Her boss at Questar asked to see the manuscript before she accepted the other offer, and they decided to publish it. *Refuge*, a bestseller, was the forerunner of Palisades, her very own Christian romance line.

As Lisa was writing her first novel, she met her husband, Tim Bergren. "From the beginning, I knew he was special and unique, and probably 'the one.' " They were engaged six months after they met, married in 1992, and three years later, their first child came along. Then three years after that, daughter number two.

The course for the next several years was set: she worked full time in publishing (after working at Multnomah, she moved to Waterbrook Press in 1996 to head up their fiction program). On the weekends, she wrote: ten novels, three novellas, two gift books, and two children's projects in nine years.

Lisa had three definite directions she felt called to: her job in publishing, her work as a writer, and her role as wife and mother. For several years, she juggled all three. People would say, "I can't believe that you do all that you do," and secretly Lisa felt gratified by the Superwoman status. Perhaps what made it possible was that she thoroughly enjoyed each of her roles, and all three used her gifts. The juggling act was not easy, but it did foster dependence on God. When Lisa prayed about it, she didn't sense she should give up any of them. "I continually asked God to move me away from writing or editing—since family obviously couldn't go!—but to make it clear to me which one it should be since I loved all three calls upon my life."

In 2000, two years after her second child was born, Lisa was feeling frazzled. While she loved her job, her writing, and her family, the mix felt like too much. She cut back her hours at her job. This helped—for a while. "My mother said I was like a new person," Lisa recalls. But Lisa continued to feel that she was stretched too thin; she could not give any of her three "callings" the time or energy she wanted to give. She continued to pray that God would make it very clear if she was to make a change.

In October of that year, God made it crystal clear. The first clue that she was dropping a few balls came the night some friends called her and asked, "Where are you?" Lisa had put the wrong date on her calendar for attending a *Riverdance* performance and totally forgot about it until the phone rang. "I was exhausted in every way. Mentally, emotionally, spiritually. I knew I was nearing the point of breakdown," Lisa says.

She looked again at her calendar and realized that she would have one month to finish the novel that was due. She knew she could not possibly write it in that amount of time, keep her job, and attend to her family—especially during the Christmas season. The editing job would have to go.

"I lived with that decision for two weeks before I said anything to my boss," Lisa says. "It was so hard. You leave jobs you hate, not jobs you love." Her Waterbrook position had given her satisfaction, stimulation, and the thrill of being part of a project from beginning to end. Yet wonderful as it was, she had to release it. When she did, she felt a tremendous relief, along with the grief of losing something she loved. There was also a sense of financial risk since Tim is self-employed. Lisa's resignation meant giving up the one steady paycheck they had. But underlying all the emotions was the knowledge that this was where God was leading, and her task was to be open to wherever he wanted her to go and whatever he wanted her to do.

"It's a matter of priorities," Lisa says. "When our priorities are in the right order, everything works so much better." Her first priority was not to be her job. "My first call is to serve God personally, then serve my family, and then thirdly, to serve God through my work."

She is realizing that when God calls you to a task, the calling may only be for a time. She had her season as a publishing executive. Now God is leading her to invest more of her energy into her other two priorities: her relationship with God and her family. She now has more time for prayer, exercise, helping her husband with his business, and her children.

She also has time to feed her imagination, to look for the small and big ways God is moving in her world. "When I take time to tune in to the child in me, when I approach my world with this sense of enchantment, wonder, and awe, it makes my world a hundred percent richer," she says. Using her imagination enriches her writing, her prayer life, time with her children—everything.

"God has given us this amazing capacity to play out things in our heads," she says. "To be able to make up characters who begin to take over the story, to be able to go to any place in the world using my imagination—it's great fun, and it's a great gift to me." When readers write to say they've been touched by her books, "it's another head shaker. All I can say is, 'Thank you, God, for using me in this way.' It's an incredible blessing. It blows me away that I get to do this for a living."

Though Lisa is where she feels she's supposed to be—for the moment, anyway—she's discovering that life with God is never static. God seems to be leading her in new directions, stretching her past her comfort zone. Before it was the juggling act that stretched her, kept her dependent on God. Now it's new opportunities. For instance, she is being asked to speak. "A year ago, when my church asked me to share my testimony, I said no. I get too nervous. I hyperventilate. I told them I would rather serve in other ways." Now Lisa is feeling God nudging her to open up to new possibilities, scary though they may be. When her church again approached her, this time asking her to preach, she said yes. "After the first five minutes, I was fine," she reports with relief.

Lisa senses she's in a new chapter of her life, one that feels much less safe, much less familiar. "I'm a planner," she says. "I like the known and safe path. But God is taking me in new directions. I'm in the process of discovering where this leads. It's both scary and exciting."

Lisa now believes that this is the way God works with most of his children. "He wants to take us to a place where we're stretched so much we *have* to depend on him. Then we discover that he is faithful, and we give him the praise. It's a lifelong process I hope I'll always welcome."

BEVERLY LEWIS

"I write out of a personal need and eagerness to share various experiences—some more fictionalized than others—that have led me to the foot of the cross. My own interest in the Amish lifestyle seems to have touched a nerve in readers. I sense a yearning in many for a simpler life, a return to traditional values. My desire is to continue to connect with my readers to the glory of God."

BEVERLY LEWIS is a member of the National League of American Pen Women, as well as the Society of Children's Book Writers and Illustrators. She has written over seventy books for every age group, from the youngest readers, to preteen series, to adult novels. She has sold over 3 million books. The Excellence in Media 2000 Silver Angel Award was granted to Lewis for her novel *The Postcard*, set in Lancaster County, the place of her birth and growing-up years, and the inspiration for many of her writings. Beverly and her husband, David, have three grown children and one grandchild. They make their home in the foothills of the Colorado Rockies.

Choices

Beverly Lewis grew up in a family where missions work predominated. Her father pioneered new churches from 1947 on, and her maternal grandfather and uncles were pastors. Her great uncle and aunt—Leonard and Ada (Buchwalter) Bolton—were missionaries to China in the 1920s. Another aunt, Beulah Buchwalter, laid down her life in Ghana, West Africa, in 1942 for the sake of the gospel. "So I come from a rich spiritual heritage, and I am thankful daily," says Beverly. Yet as she looks back on her books that have touched readers from age three to eighty and older, Beverly marvels that her words have reached so many lives.

Never having felt "called" to be a missionary or even a writer, Beverly's passion was music. As a five-year-old, she sat at the piano with her mother, making up short lyrics to the "Little Fingers" piano pieces she learned. Sometimes she practiced with such concentration that her mother set the oven timer to let her know when she should stop.

While in fifth grade, her family moved from the city to the country. Beverly recalls it as "the year there was not enough money for formal piano lessons." Heartbroken but determined, young Beverly donned her winter coat after school and headed to the cold basement, where an old upright piano sat. She practiced sometimes three and four hours a day. "I was unwavering in my purpose, not to lose any ground, even though I didn't have a teacher," she says.

She also poured out the angst of her young heart in a seventy-seven page semiautobiographical tale titled *She Shall Have Music.* Out of the depths of her "deprivation"—the loss of her musical training—the writer part of Beverly Marie (Jones) Lewis began to emerge.

Another gift Beverly felt drawn to express was teaching. As a youngster, she and her sister liked to line up their dolls and play school. From her earliest recollections, Beverly was fairly certain that whatever God ultimately led her to do in life, most likely she would be involved in some aspect of teaching.

Her real calling began, though, at the age of six, when she surrendered her life to Jesus, promising to follow him all the days of her life. Whether she was writing, teaching, or playing the piano— or later, becoming a wife and mother—Beverly's heart was soft toward the Lord. No matter what she set out to do, her goal was to please the Father.

Practically speaking, however, when God endows a person with various gifts, sometimes a choice is necessary, and that decision can be agonizing. Musician, schoolteacher, writer—what would it be? These "top three" interests tugged hard at Beverly as she considered her college major. The idea of training for the concert stage was appealing, but a highly-respected music professor remarked that if she went into teaching, she could not only support herself, but she could also pass on her love of music. His wise words impressed Beverly, and she set her sights on a Bachelor of Music Education degree.

Following college graduation in 1972, she accepted a teaching position at an elementary school located in the same district as her high school alma mater, instructing kindergarten through sixth-grade students. After getting married, she also established a home-based piano studio. She offered private instruction in voice, violin, music composition, and theory. After her first child was born, Beverly resigned from teaching but maintained her small music studio.

Yet her writing interest never waned. Though her stories seemed almost too personal for others' eyes (she hid them away), Beverly kept at her writing: journals, special letters, short stories, and essays. During high school and college, she had taken advanced composition classes. When her younger children, twins, were ten years old, she enrolled in a correspondence course at the Institute of Children's Literature, wondering if publishing might truly be within her grasp.

Slowly, steadily, she began to hone her craft, selling her work first to magazines such as *Highlights for Children, The Dolphin Log,* and *Guideposts for Kids.* Not until her twelve-year-old daughter suggested she write for "my age group" did Beverly begin to focus on writing books. Her husband also encouraged her. She began to research the marketplace and discovered just how little fiction there was at that time for eleven- to fourteen-year-old readers.

The HOLLY'S HEART series, featuring Holly Meredith of Dressel Hills, Colorado (a fictitious ski resort town), was the result. Eventually, she received a call from a Christian publishing house. "My manuscript was literally pulled from an editor's slush pile. My first contract was for four books instead of one!" says Beverly with delighted wonder. That night, within the Lewis household, the strident sounds of "To God Be the Glory"—sung by the Brooklyn Tabernacle Choir—could be heard as Beverly and her family pranced about the living room in "absolute jubilation."

Well into writing the HOLLY'S HEART series, Beverly began investigating first chapter books. She poured herself into studying controlled vocabulary and limited plot lines. "When writing for young readers, you must have the heart of a child—and learn to write succinctly," Beverly says. She saw another need in the Christian marketplace, worked hard to fill it, and a full year later an editor from a second publishing house offered her a contract for three chapter books.

After that came even more contracts. This time, for the CUL-DE-SAC KIDS and the SUMMERHILL SECRETS series, from her third publisher. Beverly was still teaching a number of music students, so her days fell into an exhausting but rewarding routine of homeschooling their twins in the morning, teaching in the studio afternoons, and writing once the children were tucked into bed, until the wee hours, "usually around two o'clock, when the house was quiet." After a few years of this taxing schedule, however, Beverly felt she wanted to make a choice between music and writing. She found it was becoming more difficult to divide her time and energy between two careers.

She and her husband, David, both involved in private music instruction, prayed for two years about what direction to take. "We asked the Lord to specifically open or close doors," says Beverly. Mixed with prayer was careful thought to priorities and reason. "I never wanted to extend my writing hours into our family time," she explains. "God had blessed me with the ability to touch hearts through my music. Yet, I loved the writing life. By balancing my deadlines, pacing myself better, I decided I wouldn't have to abandon my music students altogether. I could still be involved in church music." At the time, she was teaching several advanced piano students and decided that when the last pianist graduated from high school, she would phase out her teaching and write full time.

That day came in 1996. "I remember the senior recital of my last student as if it were yesterday. He and I played a spirited two-piano duet on stage as a finale, and it seemed as if the piece were a farewell, of sorts, to one enormous chapter of my life. Bittersweet, to say the least." She returned home to record the day in her journal in great detail. Yet as Beverly gently closed the door on her music teaching, the doors to book publishing swung even wider.

That she made the right choice is confirmed by the deep satisfaction in her heart when she sets out to write another story with a message, be it strong or subtle, that leads people to Christ. "I enjoy reading books where the main character pulls me into the pages," she says, and she prefers to write that same kind of book. "I'm not a plotter or an outliner; I always start with a strong character. The day I hear the protagonist's voice is the day I start writing the next story."

Beverly continues to write for both children and adults. Of the two genres, she finds writing for children especially rewarding and challenging. "I got my start in writing for young readers," she says, "and part of me will always be drawn to children's literature. It stretches me," she says. "If a writer can touch a child's heart for

Jesus early on, think of the people one can bring to the Lord over a lifetime!"

In some ways, Beverly is following her family's tradition of missions work—albeit in her own way, through the written word. Her Pennsylvania Dutch background has provided a rich resource of story material. Her first adult novel, *The Shunning*, was loosely based on her maternal grandmother, Ada Ranck Buchwalter, who left her Old Order Mennonite upbringing when she married. Intrigued by the story of her grandmother early on, Beverly's interest led to further research into the Plain life. Subsequently, many stories grew out of that fascination.

Beverly's heritage offers a wealth of material for writing about the struggles she's experienced herself and those of others close to her. "Though I gave my life to Jesus at a young age," she points out, "I've had my share of heartache. Christians aren't immune to the sorrow of this world. But I have experienced that God stands ready to help and guide. His grace is always sufficient as I throw myself on his mercy."

This is the hope—the message—Beverly Lewis presents to all those who wish to hear. Whether writing for children or adults, her books demonstrate that though we are weak, God is strong. His grace will carry us through every hard time.

Beverly *does* have a sense of calling, a conviction that she is precisely where God wants her to be. But that conviction is rooted in her commitment to "do all to the glory of God," and in the hard choices she has made along the way after much prayer. Like many people, Beverly has varied talents and interests—too many for one person to develop or express at one time. For years, she attempted to do it all, but the Lord led her to focus on one gift at a time.

For those who are trying to distinguish between two competing talents or interests, Beverly has some suggestions. First, bathe the decision in prayer. Talk to other wise Christians whose counsel you trust. Beverly and her husband prayed and talked things through for two years before her path became clear.

As Proverbs 16:3 says, "Commit to the Lord whatever you do,

and your plans will succeed." If you seek to honor and obey God in everything you do, he will surely guide your steps.

Be patient. Know that in the fullness of God's timing, you may yet realize all of your talents in a way only God can orchestrate. Beverly's life is still full of music—she simply doesn't instruct students any longer. Yet she continues to teach in a different way through her writing. None of her gifts have been lost. If anything, they have been expanded.

As you seek God daily, faithfully following the things you know he has put before you for now, the next step will come. And the next, and the next. Until one day, you can look back in wonder at how perfectly he directed each event of your life in his perfect timing.

PEGGY STOKS

PEGGY STOKS is the author of *Olivia's Touch, Romy's Walk* and *Elena's Song* in the ABOUNDING LOVE series, as well as novellas in five HEARTQUEST romance anthologies. Before turning to the Christian market, she published two novels and numerous magazine articles in the general market. She is also a nurse, a wife, and a mother of three children who are not yet grown.

"I would define my gift and calling as having a desire to heal. I try to write about things that real people face in an accurate and genuine manner. As my father says, getting older isn't for sissies. Life can be so difficult, and sometimes we can feel all alone in our fear, sadness, or sorrow over our sin. The thought of bringing joy and encouragement, hope and healing to readers is what keeps me going."

Juggling an "Embarrassment of Riches"

God gave Peggy Stoks a desire to heal long before she even knew that desire came from him. She graduated from high school at the age of seventeen, studied in a two-year nursing program at a community college, and by age nineteen was a registered nurse. She loved nursing. But with marriage and the needs of a growing family, she says, "It was hard to give my best to both my employer and my family. I had nothing left to give to my family."

She cut back her hours at work. She also began to think about writing. She began writing health-related magazine articles, drawing on her nursing background. She immediately succeeded in selling her articles to a local parenting magazine. During the following year of publishing nonfiction with this and other magazines, a dream was growing to write fiction. "One day it dawned on me that I was qualified to express the essence of the many life-and-death experiences [I had witnessed], and I could do that through my writing. I wondered if this was to be my 'special purpose' in life," she says. "This was in my pre-Christian days, when I had no clue about such things as callings, vocations, or God's will."

Peggy joined the local chapter of Romance Writers of America and absorbed all she could about the craft of writing. She also joined a critique group. At a large regional RWA conference sponsored by her chapter in Bloomington, Minnesota, Peggy "happened" to sit next to a senior editor of a large New York publisher. They struck up a conversation, and when the editor found out Peggy was a nonfiction writer working on her first novel, a Western historical romance, she excitedly told Peggy that her house was launching a new line of Western historical novels. The editor invited Peggy to submit a proposal. Peggy did, and two weeks later she signed a contract.

After she finished her first book, Peggy's second book proposal was quickly accepted. During the time when she was writing that book, God began working on her heart. "It still awes me to think of how involved he was in the creative process of this second novel, far before I'd said yes to him," Peggy says. She explains that she was writing for one of the steamier lines of that particular publisher, and they frequently wanted their authors to "spice up" their writing. ("My first book was plenty spicy," she admits to anyone who might wonder.)

Her second book was about a marriage of convenience, with a strong subplot about the hero's younger brother, an adolescent with Down's syndrome. Midway through writing the second book, Peggy surrendered her life to Jesus Christ. Suddenly she had a whole new perspective on what she was writing. "It was my most earnest prayer that the Lord would help me craft a manuscript that was pleasing to him, yet at the same time acceptable to the publisher"—a seemingly impossible request. Thankful that at least her characters were already married before they began to physically express their love for one another, she kept the love scenes to a bare minimum. The book went through editing without a request for "more spice," something she believes involved divine intervention, since other writers she knew were being told by that publisher to add more.

That second book began to open Peggy's eyes to the potential impact fiction has to deeply heal the hearts of readers. "I received many touching letters from readers who had a friend or loved one with Down's syndrome," she says. "This opened my eyes to the fact that readers hungered for more than engaging, entertaining stories—they responded with their whole hearts when my characters suffered through their own difficult (and not-widely-touched-upon-in-fiction) struggles. With awe and fright, I realized how much responsibility an author bears, especially an author who is writing for the Lord."

Peggy recalls a luncheon she attended at that time. Judy Baer spoke on the power books have to change people. Judy included a powerful testimony of her faith in Christ and talked about why she wrote the kind of books she did. Later, Peggy spoke with her and told her of her recent conversion. "How am I supposed to know what God wants me to do with my writing?" Peggy asked Judy.

Judy put her hand on Peggy's shoulder, smiled, and said, "Don't worry, Peggy. He'll show you what he wants you to do."

Clinging to that hope, Peggy submitted her third proposal. It was rejected. "With hindsight being what it is, I see now that God was answering my prayers about the path he wanted me to travel," she says. A surprise pregnancy caused her to step away from her writing for a few years. She used this time to study, learn, grow in her faith, and read all the Christian fiction she could get her hands on. "It was good stuff, I discovered!" she says. She thought if she was to write again, she wanted to restart her career in the Christian market.

Though she wanted to write again, she says she also "experienced total peace about the possibility of never being published again. I was thankful for the two books I had written. After all, how many people dream of writing a book, and I had published not one, but two! I told the Lord that I was willing to lay my writing aside if that was what he wished."

Other "calls" were pulling on Peggy: her vocation as wife and mother and her part-time nursing career. As she says, "There are only so many hours in a day." Her hours were quite full with the vocations she was sure of: wife, mother, nurse. So where did writing fit in to an already packed schedule?

Then came a literal "call." Peggy had met Catherine Palmer in the early 1990s, and they had continued to stay in touch over the years. Catherine knew about Peggy's spiritual journey and her desire to discern God's will for her writing. In her then-new role as consulting romance editor for Tyndale House, Catherine contacted Peggy to ask her to consider submitting a proposal for a novella for a historical Christmas anthology. "I politely thanked Cathy for thinking of me, but told her I didn't think I could manage it," Peggy says.

Two months later, Cathy again called, urging Peggy to reconsider. "I've told the editors about you, and we'd really like to see a proposal," Cathy said. "Wouldn't a project like a novella be a great way to ease back into writing?"

Peggy agonized over an answer. Was this God's way of saying "I want you to write again," or was this an opportunity she was supposed to turn down in light of her other obligations? Would she be shortchanging her family if she took on this additional responsibility? What about her job? She prayed for guidance.

"God gave me an answer in less than a week's time," she says. The first guidance came from, of all people, her carpet cleaner. "He's a wonderful, gregarious man," Peggy says. "When I explained my dilemma to him, he shook his head and said, 'Peggy, it seems to me as if you have an embarrassment of riches. I say go for it and appreciate all the wonderful things God has given you.'" The second answer came the following day at a Bible study, when she listened to a lecture on 2 Peter entitled "Your Election and Calling." The third was at Mass on Sunday when her priest delivered a penetrating homily on the Parable of the Talents.

She called Cathy back and said she'd write a proposal. "Mind you," she says, "I'd never written a novella, nor had I had any experience writing in the Christian market. I was going on blind faith!"

Assurance came from Tyndale accepting her proposals, encouraging her, and publishing her books, as well as from readers' letters. "Each reader letter is confirmation that my writing has somehow done its job and touched a particular person in whatever way the Lord has designed."

Though the confirmation is there, Peggy continues to struggle daily with issues of time and priorities. "An ongoing struggle for me is discerning what amounts of time and energy God would have me direct toward any of the given areas of my life," she says. Being blessed with "an embarrassment of riches" means knowing how to juggle them all. She points to the time and energy it takes to maintain a strong marriage and build good relationships with her three growing children. Then there are family, friend, and neighbor relationships to tend. Once a week she and a friend prayer-walk the neighborhood. She is involved in her parish, and her children are in youth activities. Not to mention the housework, the yardwork, the cooking, the laundry, and all the other responsibilities of being a homemaker. Eventually she quit her nursing job, feeling that God was calling her to be in the home at this time in her life.

Life continually throws its curve balls at her. During one period, her mother died of bladder cancer, her uncle committed suicide, and a week after that, her father was diagnosed with lung cancer and underwent the first of two major surgeries. In the midst of all this, Peggy suffered a painful herniated disk in her cervical spine.

Though each of these trials drained her, she had to keep writing. She had promised a book to her publisher. "How can I do such a thing," she cried out to God, "when I don't even feel an ounce of creativity inside me?"

On a silent retreat she had been to earlier, the word *diligence* had struck her heart in a particular way. Shortly after that, so did *perseverance.* She says, "I clung to these words through those difficult months."

Not only did God supply Peggy with those two difficult yet encouraging words, he brought to her mind the image of a long-distance runner. Step after step, mile after mile, the runner stays the race, knowing that he or she will eventually cross the finish line. "God seemed to be whispering to my soul that in the same way, if I showed up at the computer every day whether I felt like it or not, my pages would eventually turn into chapters, and those chapters into a completed book.

"I didn't have much faith," she confesses. But she did persevere and was diligent to do her part—praying for the guidance of the Holy Spirit and extending her fingers over the computer keys. Not surprisingly, God did his part. The book got finished. "Though the process was difficult, with the Lord's help I crossed the finish line," she says.

Peggy's aunt Mary speaks of "faith builders," experiences that underscore God's love and provision. Looking back on those agonizing months, Peggy realizes that they were a tremendous faith builder. "God never left, and he gave a weary, depleted woman just what she needed to complete her course."

Looking back on how God has worked in her life to bring her to this point, Peggy pinpoints many other faith builders: her friend and grandmother who prayed for her conversion, the way God had opened doors for her writing, the continuing affirmation from publishers and readers, and her experience of God's faithfulness during the dark times. She clings to these when the going gets rough. "Sometimes I wonder if I am supposed to be writing at all, but then I remember some of the reader letters I've received, the ones that make me weep. I realize that this often difficult occupation extends *far* beyond the four walls of my office, and I resolve to keep at it until the Lord sends my carpet cleaner to tell me otherwise."

CHAPTER 9

Perseverance and Hard Work

"Continuous effort—not strength or intelligence—is the key to

unlocking our potential."

— WINSTON CHURCHILL

"We can do anything we want to as long as we stick to it

long enough."

—HELEN KELLER

"Great works are performed not by strength, but by perseverance."

—SAMUEL JOHNSON

DEE HENDERSON

DEE HENDERSON is the author of two series: the O'MALLEY FAMILY series of romantic suspense and the UNCOMMON HEROES series of military romances. Her books have won a host of awards: *Danger in the Shadows* won the prestigious RITA Award, as well as Bookseller's Best Award and National Reader's Choice Award. The Reviewers International Organization voted *The Negotiator* best inspirational book of the year. She lives in Springfield, Illinois.

"My writing cracks a door for readers who otherwise aren't open to so-called 'Christian fiction.' I'm the safe front door."

The Plans of the Diligent

Dee Henderson knew she was going to be a writer before others believed in that dream. When people asked the teenaged Dee what she wanted to be, she would say, "a writer." But from the beginning, Dee had no romantic illusions about what that meant. It wasn't going to just happen. She knew it would take both time and hard work to become good enough to get published. A planner by nature, she went after her dream with a road map.

Instead of majoring in writing or literature in college, she studied to become an engineer. It was a detour, but it fit her overall plan. She figured the degree would garner her both a set of skills that would serve her writing and an income that would let her save for when she made the switch into writing as a career. She was right on both counts.

Engineering trained her in many skills that later contributed to writing: how to plan her work, manage a project, and stay on schedule (a book is a three-month project). It also honed her curiosity and taught her how to figure out how something works, which has proven invaluable when she sets out to research a book.

While she worked as an engineer, saving money and investing in books, she continued to write. She took apart dozens of books she admired to analyze why they worked. She studied the market. She wrote and wrote. "I wrote scenes when I was young; it wasn't until I was in my early twenties that I learned how to string scenes into a story. My mom says those early stories were not very good." Dee smiles. "She was right."

When her thirtieth birthday came, Dee knew she was ready to make the leap. She had an internal sense of readiness. "The desire to be a writer was overpowering." She hadn't yet sold anything, but she could see that her stories were now as good as the ones she was buying. It was time to show her work to some editors.

The transition from engineering to writing full time took two years. During that time she worked contract engineering jobs, wrote four books (one of which sold), and moved from Chicago to Springfield, Illinois. Perseverance marked that period. "I don't have a lot of gifts," Dee says, "but one is that internal sense of confidence that I'll do whatever it takes. Growing up as a preacher's kid, I learned that you have to be strategic; if you have to make a sacrifice, make it one that leads to your objective. I may have to sell the car and eat the proceeds (which I did). It may not be comfortable, but it's right."

She knew where she wanted to go, and she strategized how to get there. The goal line was very clear and very specific. This she had learned not only from engineering, but from growing up in the ministry and from her own involvement with planting churches. She kept her plan on the short term and her focus on the long term. "I assumed it would take a decade to get established, get a sense of what I could write and who my audience was," she said. She had five years worth of living expenses in the bank. She was single and planned to stay that way for a while. She moved in with her parents, who were both incredibly supportive of the dream, though at the same time they tested her to see if she was sure she was ready.

She was, despite any appearances otherwise.

Dee sold her first book the first year of her transition, 1996, and she sold about half of the stories she wrote the following year. Dee says she's a hard boss: Her job description has her in the office for fifteen hours a day, six days a week, with Sundays off. She spends half her time promoting her book in as many ways as she can think of. Though she loves the writing process itself, she doesn't kid herself. "Having others read a story is what gives it life. It's why stories are told." Plus there's the very practical aspect of wanting all her hard work to pay off, literally. "I would like to have a car again," she says.

Things were going pretty well according to plan ... until her books started winning awards. When *Danger in the Shadows* won a host of awards, including the prestigious RITA Award, Dee says it was confirmation to her mother than she could write, and a two-edged blessing for her. It was gratifying, yes, but that kind of recognition came faster than she'd planned. "It creates more internal expectations on my part," she says. "I'm there whether I want to be or not."

Five years or so into her writing career, Dee has a clearer sense of who her audience is and how to best reach them. "I'm trying to reach people who would find the gospel very attractive if they didn't have to walk into a church and be introduced as a visitor."

The characters in Dee's novels are often Christians, but they have questions and are honest enough to admit to their doubts and struggles. She tries to put the faith theme of a story in conflict with her choice of plot and characters. The theme "Fear not" was used in the witness protection thriller *Danger in the Shadows;* a cop looking at the balance between God's justice and mercy became *The Negotiator;* a forensic pathologist wrestling with the resurrection became *The Truth Seeker.* "I find the powerful stories in the intense questions."

Ultimately, she wants her books to find a place with a wider general audience. *Publisher's Weekly*'s favorable review of *The Guardian* was a major step in that direction.

Having a book reviewed by *Publisher's Weekly* was also in Dee's plan. But it came earlier than she'd projected and happened not so much from her hard work as from simply the way things turned out—God's timing, not hers. "In his heart a man plans his course," Proverbs 16:9 declares, "but the Lord determines his steps."

Dee continues to accept that her dream of supporting herself solely through her writing will take time—time and much effort. She works hard to make sure bookstores and libraries hear from her regularly. She continues to learn everything she can so that each book will be better than the last. Her Web site is full of information about release dates for her new books, comments from readers, and tips to writers. She takes every opportunity to let others know about what she's doing. "This kind of dream takes this kind of effort," she says matter-of-factly.

Dee Henderson is a planner, a doer, an analyzer—and God has used all these traits to bring her to where she is now. God's call to her is to write; the way she's expressing that call is to put her whole heart into it. "There is in the end only one decision in my plan that matters: what I decide to do with my time. Hours matter when you suddenly realize all the books you want to write cannot be done in one lifetime." Dee has committed her plans to the Lord, trusting him to bless them in his own way. He's surprised her along the way by speeding up her timetable a bit. But if good planning and hard work lead to prosperity, as Proverbs 21:5 observes, then Dee's future is secure.

God may open doors miraculously on occasion. But more often, the doors he opens are those we have knocked on persistently and diligently over a matter of time.

GILBERT MORRIS is the author of more than 165 books, most of them adult historical fiction or juvenile fiction (approximately a third of his books are for children). More than two million of his books have been sold since his first book was published in 1985. In 2001 his book *Edge of Honor* won the Christy Award in the North American Historical category. Gilbert and his wife make their home in Alabama.

"In my fiction, I strive to dramatize the gospel. It's a way of presenting the gospel that is very different from preaching; truth needs to be dramatized, not explicated."

Step by Step in Faith

Gilbert Morris lives in the world of stories as a fish lives in water. He has always read. He became a high school teacher of English and literature and later taught at the university level in the same field. He read constantly, both for his own pleasure and because it was part of what he did for a living. He didn't have to study what made stories work; he instinctively knew because of his constant exposure to stories good, bad, and mediocre.

It didn't occur to Gilbert until he was fifty-six years old, however, that maybe he himself could write a novel. In his mind, writers were an exalted breed. But because he read so many books he began to ask himself if perhaps he could write a book that was at least a little better than some of the bad ones that somehow got published. A committed Christian since the age of thirteen, he was bothered by the lack of Christian perspective in the so-called "good" novels he read. So after a day of teaching, Gilbert would retire to the typewriter and hammer out his first novel.

Once it was finished, he didn't know what to do with it. He sent it to a Christian publisher. It was rejected. He sent it out again to another publisher. Rejected again. Gilbert continued to send out his book. "I figured I would keep trying until I either succeeded or got a red light from God," Gilbert says. Twenty-six rejections followed, but Gilbert did not sense God giving him a red light yet.

At that time, in 1985, Christian publishers were publishing very little fiction. Janette Oke was beginning to prove that there was a market for fiction, but publishers still dragged their feet. Yet Gilbert Morris tenaciously hung on to his conviction that there was a place for his kind of fiction, that the world needed books in which the gospel played a prominent role. "If you feel what you're doing is of

God, then you don't quit," he says.

Finally, after twenty-some rejections, Gilbert signed his first contract with Perfection Form Company, which published *The Seven Sleepers*. The book mounted to the bestseller list and stayed on it for two years.

By now Gilbert had learned more about how to present his manuscript and approach publishers. He presented an idea for a detective series to various publishers, and Tyndale House bought it. He's been publishing ever since. The contracts that keep coming are a definite green light. In 1992, he was finally able to retire from teaching and support himself with his writing alone.

Though Gilbert does see his writing as a calling, there is very little that was or is mystical about it. He did not wake up at age fifty-six and hear a voice saying "Try writing a book." He simply began to wonder if he could do it and felt he wanted to try. He carved out the time to do it, kept at it, and then went about finding out how to find a publisher. He made mistakes. He was rejected over and over again. ("I still get rejections," he says. "It's part of a writer's life.") He kept at it, learning from his mistakes. He didn't make writing his life, though he was committed to it. And when he finally succeeded, he continued to do the hard work of sitting down and producing books.

"It's all a rather natural process," Gilbert says. "I believe this is the way it is for most of us. You have an idea, and you don't know if it's just something you want to do or if this is of God. You take a step in faith. If that works, you take another step. You keep going until God gives you a red light or slams a door in your face."

How do you know, though, if all those rejections are God's red light or if they are the normal sort of obstacles anyone faces when trying something new? Gilbert Morris says that's where prayer comes in. He didn't sense God telling him to stop, so he persevered. Rejection slips are expected obstacles for a writer, especially someone new who has never been published. If you are starting a new venture, there *will* be obstacles. They need to be faced with prayer and perseverance, in Gilbert's opinion.

In fact, prayerful dependence on God and perseverance are Gilbert Morris's formula for success in whatever calling one may have. He draws on these two resources daily. "People often ask writers what they do about writer's block," Gilbert says. "I always say there's no such thing as writer's block. Does a plumber ever say, 'I can't work today, I have plumber's block'? Of course not. Does a homemaker say, 'I won't do the dishes now, I have dishwasher's block'? No, you just do what you need to do. I go to my study, I have my work lined up, and I do it. Some days I have less inspiration than the tree outside my window. I keep going anyway. I'm sure there are pastors who don't feel inspired to preach on a given Sunday morning. But they do it anyway, because there are people who need that message."

Gilbert admits one of the biggest struggles he faces, with the number of stories he writes, is staying fresh. "That needed freshness has to come from God, and that's where prayer and depending on God come in. If there's any kind of secret to my being able to make a living at writing, it's that I keep on working and I keep on depending on God."

That's not a bad formula for any of us, no matter what it is God calls us to do. Take it step by step, depend on God, and keep going. Someday, you'll look back and be amazed at how far God has led you.

"It is my prayer for Christian fiction, and the growing number of talented novelists that continue to emerge, that together we will write works of such quality that not only will they contribute to Christian literature, but they will spark spiritual awakenings in our readers."

JACK CAVANAUGH is an award-winning author of several series of historical novels: an eight-book series of novels chronicling American history called AN AMERICAN FAMILY PORTRAIT; a two-book series featuring South Africa, *The Pride and the Passion* and *Quest for the Promised Land;* a series of four books based on the early English version of the Bible beginning with *Glimpses of Truth;* and a series dramatizing the plight of German Christians in Hitler's era, the first title of which is *While Mortals Sleep.* In addition to his writing, Jack also speaks often at conferences and other gatherings. Jack has also been the pastor of three churches in San Diego County, an editor, and a columnist.

The Long Wait

There's an old adage: If you want to be a writer you must do two things: read, read, read and write, write, write. These two strands figure prominently in Jack Cavanaugh's becoming a novelist. As a teenager, he spent his summers lost in the novels of Edgar Rice Burroughs and Herman Wouk. The writing strand developed through his preparation to become a preacher. During his junior year of high school, his church youth group went to a Youth for Christ rally and heard Rev. John MacArthur preach. "His sermons, like the literature I was reading, had a double impact," Jack recalls. "Not only was I affected by the primary purpose of the message, but also with the seed thought that God was calling me to communicate his Word just as John MacArthur was doing that night."

The ground was prepared, but in seminary the actual seed of his calling was planted. In a psychology class, Dr. John Drakeford, a prolific author himself, challenged the class. He said, "If you want to expand your ministry, not only geographically but beyond your lifetime, write." It took another year of seminary and two years of ministry before that seed would begin to bear fruit.

Three months after graduating from seminary, Jack was called to his first pastorate. Though he still wasn't writing, he enjoyed weekly opportunities to fulfill his call to ministry through the spoken word—preaching, teaching, and leading Bible studies.

But there is more to being a pastor than these three things. Jack realized that, at best, twenty percent of his time was spent fulfilling his original call to ministry while eighty percent of his time was spent taking care of administrative duties, going to meetings, equipping lay leaders, counseling, and visiting the sick. While Jack found a certain sense of satisfaction in those ministries, he also felt uneasy because his spiritual gifts had to settle for leftover time.

"My prayer at that time was that God would see fit to even out the percentages a little so that I had more time to use my gifts and fulfill my call," Jack says. He expected to see a significant change in three years. It took thirteen years. "Apparently, I needed a lot more preparation than I thought I would," he says wryly.

Along the way, though, the vision began to crystallize. He learned that Dr. Sherwood Wirt, founding editor of *Decision* magazine, had moved to the area in his retirement and started a Christian Writers Guild in San Diego. Jack began attending monthly writers critique groups. His writing ministry began in earnest.

Jack attended many Christian writers workshops over the next several years and learned much about the Christian publishing industry. He made a lot of friends, both writers and editors. One of those friends, Elaine Schulte, challenged him to enter a fiction writing contest sponsored by *CharismaLife* magazine. This was soon after the success of Frank Peretti's *This Present Darkness* began changing the landscape of Christian publishing; the magazine was looking for Peretti-type short stories. Jack entered, and out of a thousand contest entries, his story made it to the semifinals, one of the top nine stories chosen. "While I didn't win and the story never made it to print, the finish was strong enough to indicate that I was doing something right," Jack says. This, together with his strong belief in the power of the story to communicate spiritual truths, placed fiction firmly in his future goals. He began to envision the possibility of becoming a full-time novelist.

After this, Jack succeeded in getting a few nonfiction assignments published in his denominational state newspaper and his first published short story in an international ministry-related magazine. "Other than that, my efforts to sell articles and books racked up to a long string of rejections," Jack says. "A long, long, long, thirteen-year-long string of rejections." He does point to a few pinpricks of light in those days: "My rejection letters were getting glowing comments from the editors. 'Dear Mr. Cavanaugh, Wow! What a great proposal! Unfortunately, we're unable to publish your manuscript. . . .' " While others in his writing group were getting their articles published and signing their first book contracts, Jack was getting "encouraging" rejection letters.

While the rejections were mounting, Jack was also passed over for several editorial positions. Desperation led him to doubt his direction and explore any and all possible writing avenues. "I began to question my effort and abilities. I was at the point of exploring other avenues for ministry and employment, including teaching history, becoming a chaplain, applying for foreign missions, applying for a variety of denominational positions, and paying for a professional training service to help me make the transition from ministry to the business sector. God blocked every avenue."

Jack kept coming back to his heart's desire—to proclaim the Gospel through inspirational books, primarily fiction. He continued to study the craft of writing fiction, though it seemed a waste of time and effort.

The hardest rejection to take during this long drought was the constant refrain from Christian publishers: "Christian fiction just doesn't sell." It sounded like a death knell to his dream.

Jack's first break came from an unlikely source: the Sunday want ads. Christian Ed. Publishers was advertising for an editor. Though Jack's credentials—a bachelor's degree in history and master's degree in divinity—had been a deterrent to other editorial positions he'd applied for, in this case they opened the door. Art Miley, president and owner of the company, was looking for someone who could provide a sound theological foundation for their children's curriculum. As for Jack's writing qualifications, Art said, "We want to pay you for what you've been doing all these years for free."

The day-to-day involvement in editing and production sharpened Jack's writing skills. By night he continued to study fiction and prepare proposals while also continuing to pastor a local church. His job took him to writers conferences nationwide, where he was able, with Art Miley's blessing, to promote his own materials at faculty get-togethers.

His biggest break came at the Mount Hermon writers conference in 1991. At that time, the Christian fiction market had just taken off like a runaway train with the success of novels by Janette Oke, Frank Peretti, and Brock and Bodie Thoene. Suddenly publishers were looking for writers of Christian fiction. Jack met with Linda Holland, who had been enlisted by Victor Books to start a fiction line using unknown authors. Jack says, "Finally, my qualifications matched someone's needs perfectly! I was as unknown as they come."

Jack's contemporary fiction proposal was polished, and his sample chapters showed his best writing to date. Linda listened to his prepared verbal pitch, read his proposal and a few pages of his first chapter, and said, "I like it, Jack. I think I can get you a contract for this novel." At that moment, Jack says, "thirteen years of frustration and dead ends were swept away." But God's best surprise was yet to come.

In the conversation that followed, Linda told Jack that she was looking for someone to do a historical fiction series based on American history. With his history background, Jack had hoped to do such a series someday . . . someday later in his career. Jack asked what she was looking for in such a series and asked if she would mind if he submitted a proposal. The result was that the contemporary novel was shelved and Jack was offered a four novel contract for the American history series! A year later, after writing the first manuscript in the evenings after work, the series was extended to seven books. When *The Puritans* debuted, Jack Cavanaugh's writing career was finally launched.

The Puritans became a Gold Medallion finalist and winner of several local awards, both Christian and secular. This recognition, along with solid sales, finally established Jack in the Christian fiction market. When Victor Books wanted two novels a year, Jack made the break to full-time writing. When Jack informed his boss, Art Miley, of his decision to leave Christian Ed. Publishers to write full time, Art thrust his hands over his head and praised God. When Jack apologized for being with the company a short three years, Art said,

"Jack, there's nothing to apologize for. God is giving you the desires of your heart."

Jack says, "That's exactly what God has done. For the past ten years, I've been writing and speaking and preaching. God answered my prayer." The former twenty-eighty ratio is changed. Now one hundred percent of Jack's time is spent fulfilling what he sensed long ago was his calling.

Is he fulfilled? Yes, very. Is living out his calling easy? Yes and no. In exchange for the fulfillment, he puts in long hours. He's at his desk by seven in the morning, and he writes until his creative juices run out in the late afternoon. He takes breaks for lunch and dinner and when the children come home from school, but most evenings he's back in his office, doing the things that take up about half of a novelist's time: research (reading and note taking) and prewriting (plotting, drawing characters and settings, etc.).

You'll find no complaints from Jack, however. "Time passes quickly when you're doing the things you love," he says. "Besides, it took thirteen years to get here. I'm not about to waste any of this blessing."

What does the future hold for a person who has reached his goal in life? Only more and better, Jack answers. Jack senses he is part of something that God is doing through Christian fiction. He points out that in the mid–1800s a novel written by a preacher's wife changed the course of our nation. Historians list Harriet Beecher Stowe's *Uncle Tom's Cabin*—a work of fiction—as one of the causes of the Civil War because it crystallized the conscience of a nation. Jack's prayer is, "Lord, do it again!" Could a work of fiction once again crystallize the conscience of our nation and propel us into a third national revival? Only God knows. Jack says, "For my part, I'll write the stories and trust God to do the rest."

Jack had to wait thirteen long years to play his long-awaited part in what God is doing in the realm of Christian fiction. If you have a dream that seems to be going nowhere, remember Jack's thirteen years of rejections and discouragement. When you're tempted to give up, when all the doors seem closed, think of Jack Cavanaugh.

You, like Jack, are part of a bigger plan. At the right time, through prayer and perseverance on your part, the doors will swing open for you, too. If God has planted the desire in your heart, you have his word that he will fulfill it . . . in his time. In the meantime, your job is to "delight yourself in the Lord" so you will be in that place where he intends to "give you the desires of your heart" (Psalm 37:4).

CHAPTER 10

Success:
True and False

"God may allow his servant to succeed when he has disciplined

him to a point where he does not need to succeed to be happy.

The man who is elated by success and is cast down by failure is

still a carnal man. At best his fruit will have a worm in it."

— A. W. TOZER

"Fortune does not change men; it unmasks them."

—MADAME NECKER

T. DAVIS BUNN

*"I am not a minister.
I am an artist who deals
with words. I am an artist
who loves God, an
entertainer who loves God,
and my calling is to be the
best artist and entertainer
I can be."*

T. DAVIS BUNN was raised in North Carolina, taught international finance in Switzerland, worked in Africa and the Middle East, and was named managing director of an international business advisory group based in Dusseldorf. He is the author of fourteen bestselling novels. T. Davis Bunn has won numerous awards for his writing, and his books are frequent book club selections. One of his latest books, *The Great Divide,* was published simultaneously by Doubleday and Waterbrook Press and won acclaim in both the Christian and secular arenas. He and his wife, Isabella, now divide their time between Melbourne Beach, Florida, and Oxford, England.

Two Kinds of Success

At age twenty-eight, T. Davis Bunn had achieved the kind of success that few even dream of attaining. He was running a subsidiary of an international company, he traveled to three countries a week, and he was making more money than he could ever spend. He was achieving all his goals at lightning speed. Like many people, he had unconsciously assumed that when he reached his goals, he would be happy.

"What I discovered as I looked beyond arriving at my goals," Davis says, "was that everything on the outside was empty. All that 'success' had no impact on the inner turmoil I was feeling all the time." He was living in Dusseldorf at the time and began attending church and a Bible study made up of Germans and Americans. Though it's difficult for him to pinpoint any particular moment when he gave his life to Christ, he did notice changes as he began to pray and study the Bible.

One day Davis listened to some tapes of Josh McDowell lecturing at an American college. Josh said that a question he is often asked by unbelievers is how he can be so certain God exists. The most powerful and clearest indication of the presence of God to Josh McDowell was that he could turn around and look back to where he had been six months ago, and he knew the transformations could not have been from his own doing. "That's exactly how I felt about my own life," Davis Bunn says. He realized that the Holy Spirit was at work in his life.

Two weeks after this realization, Davis set out for yet another set of business meetings. This one was in Frankfurt, about two hundred miles south of his home. He drove to the meetings, met up with some colleagues, and waited in the hotel lobby while the others went up to their rooms to get ready for dinner. His thoughts turned to the story that had been growing inside him for a few weeks. He had some time to kill; why not try to set the story down on paper?

It turned out to be a spiritual and occupational turning point. "Within the hour I knew I was willing to listen to what God was offering me." All his business doings, his worldly success, had rested on Davis doing his own will. It had proved as empty as the wind. Now it seemed as if God was offering him a gift, something that would fulfill him. "It was like falling in love," Davis says.

Yet Davis had never written anything before. Apparently the gift had lain dormant, awakened only when he began living his life in the context of faith. His whole inner life was shifting. The social whirlwind of international commerce meant less and less to him. He began to withdraw and even found a monastery that served as a retreat. There he began to write in earnest and to study ancient Christian texts. Having starved his inner life while he amassed his outward successes, he was now hungry to learn as much as possible about silence, prayer, and meditation. He set about to learn discipline, something he felt he'd lacked until that time. He woke at five in the morning as often as he could to write, shooting for a goal of twenty hours a week of writing. He would hit this goal three weeks out of four. Still he was traveling, still he was involved in his business. But now he had something of his own to balance the demands that had seemed so empty before; now he had his faith in Christ and his writing.

The writing itself took faith as well as discipline. Davis points out that fulfilling one's calling usually does mean facing the seemingly impossible obstacles. For him to write, he had to find time when there seemed to be no time. He was traveling three days a week; "my time was not my own," he says. Realizing he could not rely only on time in his "prayer and writing room" to write, he learned how to write in taxicabs and airports and hotel lobbies.

No one took his writing seriously except a woman named Isabella, who eventually became his wife. Still he kept writing, until he met the ultimate test of his commitment to his passion.

A few months after meeting Isabella, Davis was offered the job of a lifetime: to be president of an international company based in Holland. But there was one catch. He would have to give up the writing. "I want you body and soul," his potential boss said.

Davis's family said, "When do you start?" The notion of refusing such a lucrative offer was unthinkable to them.

By this time Davis had been writing for eight years. It was as much a part of him as breathing. How could he give it up and not suffocate? Yet, if God really wanted him to write, wouldn't he have given Davis some sign by then? He had written seven books in eight years, and not one had been published. Was he fooling himself? Perhaps he should stick to business, which he was obviously good at.

But business did not fulfill him. He had already tasted all that worldly success had to offer.

Isabella, who had herself just been offered a good job in The Hague, perceived the real issues. She told Davis, "We can take our jobs, buy a big mansion, have his and her Mercedes, and be miserable for the rest of our lives. Give writing another chance, if that's what you really want to do. And if you do, I would be willing to be your agent."

In wrestling over his decision, Davis realized he had never really put his writing on the altar, had never completely entrusted it to God with a willingness to walk away from it if that's what God wanted. In the beginning he had this sense that writing was from God, but then he had clutched it to himself. It was his passion, and he wanted to write more than anything else. Could he put all that passion and desire on the altar and leave it with God?

He knew he didn't really have a choice. "I knew I had to be honest. I had already seen what a mess I made of my own life when I controlled it. I wanted to write more than anything, and I knew if I couldn't I would never feel fulfilled. Yet if this was a selfish desire, I had to be willing for God to take it away." On the way to the airport for yet another business trip, he mentally put the writing on the altar. "I felt I had died," he says. "In the next few days, I had this sense of having attended my own funeral."

While praying on the plane trip back, Davis received not a vision but a feeling of approaching that altar on which lay his ultimate sacrifice. There he met a God of love. "I did not have the sense that the writing was being given back to me, but that the creative gift was magnified for having been done in faith from that point on."

Davis had his answer. He told his would-be boss he would accept the job on the condition that he be given six months to complete his current manuscript. No dice. He kept his old job and married Isabella.

One month after they married, Davis received his first publishing contract. It was a confirmation of sorts. For the next two years, he continued working his old job and writing on the side. Isabella had quit her job and was consulting. Their aim was for her to begin graduate studies in London as soon as Davis was able to support them with his writing. Two years later, with his fourth manuscript accepted by Bethany House, they moved to London, where Isabella began graduate studies.

The next two years were quite a contrast to the life they could have had if they had taken those two lucrative jobs. Instead of a mansion and his and her Mercedes, they lived in a small flat and didn't even own a car or television! "Our income had been cut by eighty-five percent with Isabella in graduate school and our living on my writing income. Finances were very tight. Yet it was easier than we had expected. Only with God's presence could we have both been so comfortable with such a drastic change."

T. Davis Bunn and his wife now had what no money could buy: faith in God, faith in each other, and work that meant something to them—work that was in line with the way God had designed them.

T. Davis Bunn experienced both forms of "success": the kind defined by making lots of money, and the kind defined by doing what he was made to do. He found that outward prosperity without inward resources was empty. Yet pursuing the path of inward satisfaction was in some ways more difficult. The training, the self-discipline, the pressing on when almost no one else believed in him, tested his sense of calling to the full. Even when the confirmations come—getting published, hitting the bestseller lists, and winning awards—Davis has the sense that his gift is incomplete. Each book is a new challenge to do better, to hone his skills as a writer.

Yet, though harder, this way of life is by far the richer. "Life is a lot more interesting because I have far to go," he says.

Perhaps this is true success: doing what you love to do and having others receive your gifted passion. It may take a while for the world to acknowledge the gift; hang in there! Leave the results up to God as you faithfully develop your gift. As T. Davis Bunn says, "It's dangerous to use physical success to confirm whether you are succeeding in God's eyes. I know someone who also wants very passionately to write, yet she has a handicapped child and may never be able to give what it takes to become a professional writer. I feel for such people—I really do. I have been fortunate that I have been able to make my living doing what I love to do. But I don't feel any more a success in the eyes of God because I've succeeded in the world than my friend who may never get published."

In the end, each of us plays to an audience of One. And he is the one who pronounces true success and failure.

LIZ CURTIS HIGGS

"My calling—and my greatest delight—is to encourage women to embrace the grace of God and celebrate their life in him with JOY!"

LIZ CURTIS HIGGS is well known as both a speaker and prolific writer. After ten years in radio, Liz became a professional speaker, and has presented humorous, encouraging programs in all fifty states and four foreign countries. In 1995, Liz received the highest award for speaking, the Council of Peers Award for Excellence, becoming one of only three dozen women in the world named to the Speaker Hall of Fame. Liz is also a bestselling author. She has written many nonfiction books for women, including her award-winning *Bad Girls of the Bible* and its companion book, *Really Bad Girls of the Bible,* and four PARABLE SERIES books for children, which were also awarded the ECPA Gold Medallion Award for Excellence. Her novel *Mixed Signals* was a Romance Writers of America RITA finalist for both Best First Novel and Best Inspirational Novel.

Signposts of Joy

In one "lighter than usual" month, Liz Curtis Higgs and her husband, Bill, kept track of everything that came through her office. There were 43 requests to speak, 118 orders for books and tapes, 126 letters from readers ("Yes, I really do answer them all," Liz says), 255 requests for her newsletter, 34 requests from publishers, 35 requests from speaking clients, and 15 media interviews. "I have to have a real clear vision of what I'm supposed to do, because I could be so distracted," Liz says.

Such a mind-boggling list of opportunities could stymie anyone who wasn't sure of her calling. But Liz is sure. For now, anyway, she is called to write. To write fiction, specifically. It's what she's always wanted to do, indeed what she began doing for the sheer joy of it at age ten. But in the thirty-odd years between then and now, the Lord has taken her on a path with many twists and turns, a path strewn with opportunities and a few obstacles and sidetracks. The story of how she came to this point is full of transitions, yet the seeds for everything she ended up doing were already sprouting in childhood.

As soon as Liz could read, she began to write. "My childhood scrapbooks are stuffed with stories, poems, and descriptions of funny incidents—much like the material I write for publication today," she says. She wrote her first full-length novel at age ten—a takeoff on the Nancy Drew mysteries, except her heroine was Betsy Lane. By the time she was seventeen, she'd written ten Betsy Lane mysteries and one adolescent romance ("lots of hand-holding and one stolen kiss"). Her friends passed around Liz's notebook novels, and several teachers also read them and encouraged her to pursue writing.

"When God calls, he also equips," Liz says. Though she was not spiritually sensitive enough to hear God's "call" at the time, she did see the evidence of being equipped. "I always encourage those who long to know what God wants them to do to examine those things they did as a child—naturally, effortlessly, joyfully," she says. "Calling, passion, and talent all come in a God-shaped package. Sometimes it's not apparent in childhood but comes all at once in adulthood," she adds. "Either way, it's a package deal—calling and equipping come together and come from God."

Public speaking was another avenue Liz was equipped to do early on. As a child, her father monitored her speaking. He'd say, "If you can write well and speak well, every door will be open to you." She studied voice, and for a long time dreamed of becoming a professional singer. At one point, she had to face reality. "I was an okay singer," she says, "but there were other people out there who sang much better." She had to let go of that to fully grab hold of what her true focus should be.

Liz was equipped in writing and in speaking, but hearing God's call meant being in tune with God. During her college years and through most of her twenties, Liz was more in tune with the world than with God. "It wasn't until I was twenty-seven and in the pit that I looked up and saw God's hand outstretched to me," she says. "When I came to know God, I began asking for the first time, 'God, what do you want me to do with my life?'"

At the time, Liz was a radio personality on WAKY in Louisville, which had an oldies format, where she did an upbeat morning show. She had met God and wanted more than anything to tell others about him. That meant she was supposed to be a missionary, right? She applied to a mission board, but the board said, "You don't have to go anywhere. You have a mission field in your radio listeners. You know their culture better than most Christians." Liz wanted to serve God on the foreign mission field—but God said stay put. "I was despondent," Liz recalls.

But then came the invitations to speak in churches, to share her testimony. More people asked her to come and speak. They even asked her to speak again, which meant preparing more material. And so her speaking career was launched, and she left radio. "Radio was definitely a calling, for a time, and so was the speaking," she says. "Speaking will probably always be part of who I am and what I do. There is something wonderful that happens between a speaker and an audience."

After ten years or so, the speaking led to writing as publishers approached her. She wrote many nonfiction books and continued to speak—a grueling schedule of 120 speaking engagements and two books a year. She read voraciously on her many plane trips, turning more often than not to fiction.

After a while, she began to wonder if she should try her hand at fiction. On one eight-hour plane trip to Germany, she decided it was time. She opened up her laptop and began to write. "It was wild—the story just exploded in my head," Liz said. She grabbed every moment she could during that trip to write, and she found she loved it. She realized that even if nobody ever published what she wrote, she loved the whole process of making up characters and putting them into situations and seeing what happened. For her, it was pure recreation.

But would it ever be more? To answer that, she had to take a courageous step and show someone what she wrote. She showed the novel to her husband, who is also her business partner. She knew he would be kind but honest. After reading her story, with tears in his eyes he told her, "You have the gift." Liz also showed it to other writers. She knew this was a turning point. If she were to turn to writing more fiction, she would have to take some risks. She knew she would need to be home more, both for the fiction writing, which takes longer and is more intense than writing nonfiction, and for her family. "I abandoned myself to God," she says. She told God she would do whatever was necessary. She also asked that if this was what he wanted her to do, that he would open the doors. "Not everyone believes that a nonfiction author can do fiction," she explains. "One publisher told me that in their experience, nonfiction authors did not make good fiction authors."

Doors did open for Liz's fiction, and she feels she has come home. Not that she hasn't fought some battles along the way. She had to fight to get some of her children's books published—the same books that went on to win awards. Her approach to *Bad Girls of the Bible* was also rather unusual—Bible study and fiction combined? Yet Liz felt strongly that this was the way God wanted her to write these books, and her publisher gave her the freedom to do so. "The fact that it was a Gold Medal finalist in the Bible study category shows you God's sense of humor," Liz says.

Liz sees her current calling as writing fiction. It is the riskier road to take for a number of reasons. First, it's not as financially certain as speaking or even writing nonfiction. "But I was never motivated by money anyway, so that's not a big factor" in decision making, Liz says. The bigger risk was emotional—the self-doubt that comes when trying something new. Because Liz already had a following, she wondered how she would take it if readers told her that her novels were terrible. "It's not like I had the luxury of having written five terrible novels that were in the drawer," she notes ruefully. As an already established author, she was able to get a contract—now she just had to deliver. "Would my nonfiction readers and audiences like the 'new Liz,' or shake their heads and say, 'She's lost it now'?" That pressure to deliver didn't let up after the first successful book, either. "I feel that each book has to be at least as good as the last one, or I'm letting my readers down," Liz explains.

But the added pressure does not deter Liz, because she's sure of her calling. In fact, she believes that sometimes it's God who puts us through pressure and trials to test our resolve and to keep us dependent on him. Just because you hit a roadblock, it doesn't mean God wants you to find another path. If you are on the right road, you will experience a certain joy in the journey itself, even if the road becomes rocky. Liz has found that when she's doing what God made her to do—and for her now, that means writing fiction—then there will be a certain joy that gives strength. "I keep thinking of the Scripture from Hebrews about Jesus, 'who for the joy set before him endured the cross,' " Liz says. "If there's this overriding sense of joy, mission, and passion, then that endeavor is of God. I have found that if something is very stressful, it's of Liz, but if it's of God, it flows." Not that it's always going to be easy, but there will be "moments of pure joy along the way."

The joy is the sign that she's on the right road; the joy is the energy that keeps her going. Keeping the joy requires always listening to God, sensitive to when he might lead in yet another direction. That's where prayer comes in—constant prayer. "I think of it like when you're logged on to your computer," Liz says. "You can log on to the Internet and stay there, and when an email message comes through, you can click on it and immediately read it. That's 'praying without ceasing' mode; you're always ready to receive any messages from God. One alternative to that is to not be logged on continually, to tune in whenever you have something to say. In that case, you might get too busy and miss an important message. Another alternative is to have to reboot every time. Me, I'd rather stay in constant touch."

Maintaining a "listening mode" is what keeps Liz sane when hundreds of requests to speak come in, when the opportunities and pressures overwhelm her. Not all of us are faced with the work load or stresses Liz confronts daily. But all of us must search for and then embrace those opportunities we are uniquely called and gifted to undertake. Many opportunities may call, but only a few can be chosen. Liz's advice: "Choose what gives you joy. The surest sign that I am called to write is this: I am happiest when I'm writing. The sense of rightness and satisfaction is overwhelming. This is not to say it is always *easy*, but it is always *right*."

JERRY B. JENKINS

"Fiction was always my first love. Jesus himself taught with fiction (the parables were clearly Truth told in fictitious stories)."

JERRY B. JENKINS is the author of dozens of books—he stopped counting at a hundred, he says. His books range from autobiographical "as-told-to" stories of sports figures such as Walter Payton, Hank Aaron, Orel Hershiser, Nolan Ryan, and Mark Singletary, to books on marriage and family, to fiction for both adults and children. In 2001 Jerry purchased the Christian Writers Guild. Of course, his most famous work is the LEFT BEHIND series, which was conceived by Tim LaHaye and for which Jerry serves as novelist. That series has become the bestselling series in the world and an unparalleled publishing phenomenon.

The Test of Success

Jerry Jenkins' direction in life began as what he thought was an unfortunate detour. In high school his goal was to become a professional baseball player, but then he was injured playing football. He began sports writing for the school paper to stay close to the sports scene, and he quickly realized he had found his niche. "I believe the injury and my realization that baseball was not my future were God's way of getting my attention," Jerry says. "I was raised in a Christian home and was never a rebel, but baseball was way ahead of my faith as my first love."

During summer camp at age sixteen, Jerry felt a definite call to full-time Christian service. "I went forward assuming, with trepidation, that I would have to study and train for the pastorate or missionary work," he remembers. "It took me a while to realize that God would call me to that for which he had gifted me."

The gift God has given him is writing. "It's my only gift," Jerry says—not to appear falsely modest, but to emphasize that because it is his only gift, he has felt an obligation to exercise it to the fullest. He has worked hard, averaging more than five books a year for twenty-five years.

His writing career officially started in 1971. He was twenty-one, a newlywed, when he caught a glimpse of himself in a plate glass window. "I saw myself in a suit and tie and realized I was a grown-up," Jerry says. "It was time to answer the call. I began searching for work in Christian writing." He got a job as a Sunday school paper editor at Scripture Press. "I well recall starting at Scripture Press in 1971 and feeling great joy that I could exercise my gift as an answer to that teenage call," Jerry says.

He went on to edit a Christian version of *TV Guide*, then was hired at Moody Bible Institute as the editor of *Moody* magazine. He has worked there for more than twenty-six years, moving from magazine editor to magazine publisher, to vice-president of publishing—all the while writing books on the side. He talked his way into three hardback "as-told-to" autobiographies (Hank Aaron, Chicago Bulls coach Dick Motta, and Chicago Bulls general manager Pat Williams). He worked on all three during the same year, and no one but his wife knew he was writing them. They came out within months of each other. "Overnight, it seemed, I was widely published," Jerry says.

All the time Jerry worked full time at Moody, he had to confine his writing to evenings. He committed to doing no writing or office work from the time he got home to the time his three sons went to bed. So from 1975 until 1990, his book writing was done between nine and midnight. It was that sense of exhilaration and desire to write that kept him returning to the computer night after night. "Though I was exhausted and not a night person, in some strange way I was motivated and productive," he says. "I had no choice, if I wanted to continue to write. And I wrote without guilt because I was not shutting out my family to do this. The time constraint kept me focused and was a deterrent to writer's block."

Jerry's first major crossover success was Orel Hershiser's autobiography, which came out in 1989 and debuted at number five on the *New York Times* bestseller list. He later made the list with Nolan Ryan's life story and Billy Graham's memoirs (with which he assisted).

In 1990, Jerry became a writer-in-residence at Moody and began writing full time from home. Remaining attached to Moody is a connection he treasures: "Moody is my proudest association."

Finally he could focus all his energies on writing. His interests were wide ranging, from sports, to marriage and family, to children's books. Though many of his books were nonfiction, Jerry says that fiction was always his first love. "I wrote nonfiction to pay the bills, in the hopes that the fiction would hit." Before *Left Behind*,

Jerry had written twenty-two adult novels and thirty-six children's novels.

Some time after signing on with the Alive Communications literary agency, his agent, Rick Christian, approached him about a project. Rick explained that another client of his, Tim LaHaye, had an idea about what might happen if an airline pilot had a lot of people on his plane suddenly disappear because the Rapture had occurred and he had been left behind. Tim had been looking for a novelist to write such a book. Rick and Tim had prayed about the situation, and Jerry came to Rick's mind as the perfect candidate.

Jerry and Tim met to discuss the possible project—and they clicked right away. Tim says, "We were soul mates spiritually and in the way we read Scripture." Tim gave Jerry a flowchart with the events based on prophecy that would need to be covered in the novel. Jerry took off with the idea, as excited about it as Tim, and applied his finely-honed writing skills to Tim's outline.

The rest, as they say, is history. The LEFT BEHIND series did hit—phenomenally. Tim LaHaye waited ten years with his idea and Jerry Jenkins spent nearly twenty-five years honing his craft, but their patience and hard work finally resulted in a series that has made publishing history. It is the bestselling series in the world. The adult titles combine to sell a million copies a month, and ever since the seventh book, *The Indwelling*, soared immediately to the number one spot on all the crossover bestseller lists, each new book has followed suit. This is especially amazing since at least a third of the books' sales are not counted because Christian retailers are not included in the tracking.

"These kinds of figures go way beyond any writer's ability," Jerry says. "The numbers are so huge, I can't dream of taking any credit. It's way too overwhelming to be anything but a God thing."

That God is using Jerry's gift for words for ministry is unmistakable. Letters from readers pour in, testifying to the spiritual impact of the books. "More than ever, we're hearing of people coming to the Lord," Jerry says. He and Tim LaHaye stand in awe of how God is using their words.

That alone is motivation to keep writing—but it's also pressure. Readers clamor for the next book as soon as the latest is out, but it's difficult to write two big novels a year. After publishing two novels a year in 1999 and 2000 (*Apollyon* and *Assassins* in 1999 and *The Indwelling* and *The Mark* in 2000), Jerry and Tim have gone back to publishing one novel per year until the series ends. Jerry wants every book to be better than the last.

When Jerry needs to get serious about writing, he holes up in "the cave"—an office with no phone lines, no access to the Internet . . . no distractions. "The only thing I can do in that room is write or read . . . or sleep," Jerry adds with a chuckle. "If I didn't have a room in which to just write, all the other distractions would pull me off course."

One of his biggest distractions is reading and responding to his email, as he gets more email messages every day. Jerry used to answer every message that came to him directly, though he knew the day would come when he couldn't respond so personally. "It was getting to be a full-time job, just to answer the emails," he says. Though he dreaded the day when he'd have to send stock answers, by the end of 2000, that day had come.

On top of the pressure most novelists would feel under these circumstances, there is the added spiritual oppression Jerry feels every time he enters "the cave" to write another LEFT BEHIND book. "Weird things happen," he says. "Computer glitches. Illness. Unexplained fatigue. Once, three of the subcontractors working on my office building got in car wrecks. I always feel tremendous mental and physical pressure when I'm writing this series. It feels like front-lines work, spiritually speaking." To counteract the oppression, Jerry asks a few close friends and family members to pray for him during these writing periods.

He also depends on close friends to keep his perspective straight: "I have a few friends whom I've told that if they detect that I'm letting [success] get to my head, they can punch me out," Jerry says.

Pressure aside, there are certain fun aspects of being "the most famous writer no one's ever heard of," as Jerry refers to himself. Jerry had always dreamed of seeing a stranger reading one of his books. "It never happened to me before, but with the LEFT BEHIND series, it's happened literally hundreds of times," he says. He tells how he has seen people on an airplane reading one of the books, and he has asked them what it's about. The person tries to describe the story. At some point Jerry will say, "People tell me I look like the guy on the back cover." The person will look and say, "Yes, you do, sort of." And then Jerry will say, "Well, I really am the author," and relish the response. (Once someone said, "Glad to meet you, Mr. LaHaye"!)

Needless to say, Jerry Jenkins doesn't need to write another book in order to pay the bills. But he says he's never been motivated by money. "Neither Tim LaHaye nor I grew up in families where success was defined by money," he says. Ministry was always more important. Now that he's been put to the test, he's pleased to find that ministry truly is what motivates him.

Not that he doesn't enjoy the freedom to, say, hop a plane and visit his son and daughter-in-law whenever he wants. Or to be able to design his own office building, with its full racquetball court and basketball court. But Jerry is also aware of the dangers of wealth. "I'm glad [this kind of success] happened at this stage of my life rather than twenty years ago, when it might have turned my head," he says. "I see [money] as dynamite: It has a lot of power, but it also can be dangerous. I want to continually remember that this is not mine and that it does not make me independent of a need for God. We have to answer for every dime we have and what we do with it." Jerry adds that his coauthor has been a wonderful model of what a good steward is. "I have been inspired by the LaHayes and how incredibly generous they have been. They enjoy what they have, but they don't hoard or flaunt money or spend it all on themselves."

Jerry says that he's heard all his life that wealth will not change you; it will just magnify the person you really are. He has found that to be true. "While there are clear benefits to the freedom excess allows, you still have to watch what you eat, stay in the Word, keep your temper, and try to put others first. Money doesn't make any of that automatic."

Nor does wealth mean he will slow his writing pace. With several more books to finish both in the LEFT BEHIND and the LEFT BE-HIND: THE KIDS series, Jerry continues to be immersed in the subject. But his interest hasn't waned a whit. For one thing, the books are moving toward a great climax: the return of Jesus Christ. For another, there are always new characters to invent, new surprises to encounter as he writes. Jerry is not the type of writer who plans exactly what is going to happen in each book. Tim LaHaye gives him the biblical outline, but how the characters react in those situations unfolds on the page as he writes. "Discovering what happens is as much fun for me as it is for the readers," Jerry says. "I don't kill my characters off; I find them dead." Once the story is set in motion, characters and plot take on a life of their own.

This is what keeps Jerry Jenkins writing—the joy of the act itself and the deep fulfillment that comes from knowing that God is using his books to touch many lives with the Gospel. Every day he feels a profound gratitude for all he's been given, even before the success of LEFT BEHIND. "I have lived a writer's dream for decades and feel blessed beyond what anyone deserves," he says.

Perhaps he doesn't deserve it any more than the next writer. But no one can say that Jerry Jenkins hasn't paid his dues. He continues to work hard at his craft, enduring the unique pressures of success, spurred on by a sense of mission: to use his gift for words to call others to live in the light of the imminent return of Jesus Christ. That's success in the eyes of the only One whose opinion matters.

CHAPTER 11

God's Gracious Ways

"There is no event so commonplace

but that God is present within it."

— FREDERICK BUECHNER

"God is as creative in how he breaks into our lives

as he is in the original creation."

—LUCI SHAW

DIANE NOBLE

DIANE NOBLE is the award-winning, bestselling author of a dozen novels, three novellas, and three nonfiction books. Two of her novels, *When the Far Hills Bloom* and *Distant Bells*, were 1999 finalists for the prestigious RITA Award. Diane lives in the mountains of southern California with her husband, Tom.

"I love to help my readers and others discover, through my storytelling, who they are in Christ— unique and beautiful and gifted beyond measure."

Led in the Path of Mercy

When God asks us to do a particular work to help him accomplish his purpose, he graciously works within the unique strengths, interests, and even weaknesses he has placed within us. As Diane Noble looks back on how she became a writer, she marvels at two things: that she can see a pattern even from childhood, and that God worked within the framework of her own personal limitations.

Diane fell in love with words, stories, and images when she began reading at the age of eight. Her parents had many good books on the bookshelves, and she quickly progressed from reading young adult novels to adult fiction. In high school, she was required to turn in an essay every Monday morning to her English teacher. "I remember Sunday afternoons with my father, sitting and talking about ideas. He loved reading, was very articulate, and he was patient with me. Sometimes the teacher gave us subjects to write about, sometimes we could make up stories. That was the first time I realized what a joy it was to play with words and put words down on paper," she says.

Later in college, Diane couldn't settle on a major and dabbled in a variety of subjects that caught her interest: psychology, history, music, art, and finally English, especially creative writing. She laughs now at how God uses even those years of indecision. She uses her studies in each of those "majors" as she develops her characters and plots. "Many of my characters are artists or lovers of art and music. And of course, my dabbling in psychology comes in handy in my romantic suspense plots," she laughs.

At age eight, Diane gave her heart to the Lord. "Through the years I felt a nudging, that there was something special God had for me to do. A calling. I just didn't know what it was." The thought of becoming a writer intrigued her, but at the same time it seemed like reaching for the stars. "When I was young, I identified with Jo March in *Little Women*. She was passionate and spirited and . . . a writer! I wanted to be just like her. But as I grew older, it was Louisa May Alcott who became my hero. I was in awe of her. I had a passion for writing and dreamed of someday writing my own stories . . . but I couldn't imagine how I could become an author."

It wasn't until twenty years later that the two things came together—her love of reading and writing, and the call to serve God through that means. God nudged her along step by step, using each season in her life to move her there. He also used her limitations. Diane explains, "I'm not at all aggressive. I don't take rejection well. God knows this about me. He placed people in my path to get my attention. People I never would have had the nerve to approach on my own." She laughs again. "People such as editors, agents, even author friends to encourage me."

As a young mother, she was so filled with joy over the miracle of birth that she wrote about her feelings and experiences. At the encouragement of an editor on staff with the magazine *Psychology for Living*, Diane began writing a monthly column about her experiences as a new mom. Her articles hit a responsive chord among other young mothers. They also opened another door. One day as she was dropping off her article, Clyde Narramore, editor in chief of the magazine, asked her to step into his office to meet Bob DeVries, who was acquisitions editor for Zondervan at the time. Bob had read her columns and told her, "We have been looking for someone to write a gift book for expectant and new mothers. Would you like to submit something?"

With that encouragement, Diane submitted her proposal. Soon her first book was in print, and then another.

By the mid–1980s, her longing to write fiction grew. Her children were now in school, and she was working as a freelance writer, penning magazine articles and grant proposals for nonprofit organizations. She began to study the craft of fiction. She began her first novel. Now she was writing day and night: nonfiction for her job, fiction at night for herself.

In the mid–1990s, Diane met Lisa Bergren through a mutual friend. Lisa was beginning the Palisades romance line for Multnomah at that time. The two women chatted about ideas, and Lisa encouraged Diane to write up some proposals. "Again," Diane says, "God had put someone in my path to nudge me along." Diane submitted her proposals, and soon she had her first three-book contract for Christian fiction.

"I loved writing fiction from a Christian perspective," Diane says. "I felt I had come home." There was one problem, though: She still had a demanding full-time job as a staff writer and editor for World Vision International, the Christian relief agency, a job that required travel. She loved that job, too, but wondered about doing both.

For a while she *did* both. She decided to use a pen name, Amanda MacLean, for her fiction. "I felt at the time that I needed a separate persona for the fiction," Diane explains. "I was doing two vastly different kinds of writing—writing about abject poverty in the 'Two-Thirds World' [more often called the Third World] and storytelling in the form of historical romance. Using a pen name helped me separate the two very different writing worlds."

Again, God in his mercy and kind personal care intervened. Within months after Diane signed her three-book contract, World Vision announced that the company would be relocating to Seattle. Diane and her husband prayerfully considered whether to uproot and move from southern California. But Tom, a teacher at a local community college, was at a point in his career where he could not move. "It became clear to us that the door was opening for me to move into full-time fiction writing," Diane says. "I knew it was God's call." Diane finished five Palisades books using her pen name and then began using her true name.

Looking back, Diane marvels at how God led her each step of the way, from the first early yearnings to write to published author of more than a dozen books, ten of them fiction.

Several years ago Diane added her personal dialogue with God to Jeremiah 1:5–9:

God says, "Before I formed you in the womb I knew you, before you were born I set you apart. . . ."

Jeremiah responds, "Ah, Sovereign Lord . . . I do not know how to speak; I am only a child." Diane's paraphrase: "I do not know how to write, I am so inexperienced."

And the Lord replied, "Do not say 'I am only a child.' [Do not say you are inexperienced.] You must go to everyone I send you to and say whatever I command you. Do not be afraid . . . for I am with you. . . ."

Jeremiah concludes, "Then the Lord reached out his hand and touched my mouth [touched my heart] and said to me, 'Now, I have put my words in your mouth [heart].' "

That was the beginning of the call for Diane. It came through God's Word impressed personally on her heart. It grew as she persevered in learning her craft. At the right time, God opened doors. Mindful of Diane's strengths—and weaknesses—God led her to people in the publishing world who liked her ideas and encouraged her on to the next step. "When I look at how he has led me," Diane says, "I have to rejoice. He works with each of us in such different ways to get us on the path to follow his call, according to who we are inside and what our gifts are, and the challenges we have to overcome."

Each person's relationship with God is individual, personal. He rarely works in exactly the same way twice. But this he does consistently: he mercifully fits the call and the means to the unique personality, circumstances, weaknesses, and strengths of each individual. Never forget God's first call is to a relationship with him. As you respond to that primary call, he gently leads you in the path he has created just for you. You'll know the way, because the shoes he gives you will fit exactly, the signposts will seem written just for you, and all along the way joy will spur you on.

PENELOPE J. STOKES

"When I write fiction, I'm not trying to persuade anyone to think as I do; I'm simply creating characters—memorable ones, I hope—who live out their own doubts, struggles, victories, and faith in a manner the reader can identify with. Fiction is story, not sermon; it's people, not propaganda. For me, the calling is to live in connection with God and then allow that connection to flow out of me into what I write."

PENELOPE J. STOKES has published a number of both fiction and nonfiction books. She holds a Ph.D. in literature from the University of Mississippi, and wrote *The Complete Guide to Writing and Selling the Christian Novel.* She has also written *Faith: The Substance of Things Unseen* and a number of devotional books, two of which have been Gold Medallion finalists (*Simple Words of Wisdom* and *Beside a Quiet Stream*). But her real love is writing fiction. Her trilogy of World War II novels—*Home Fires Burning, Till We Meet Again,* and *Remembering You*—was inspired by the story of her parents' experience. Two other novels, *The Blue Bottle Club* and *The Amethyst Heart,* have been acclaimed by both readers and critics.

Connecting with God

Penelope J. Stokes was born to be a writer. In her case, both nature and nurture sealed her destiny. Her mother was an English teacher who read Faulkner for fun and put the young Penny to bed at night with Edgar Allan Poe stories. ("My friends say this explains a lot," she says.) Her father was a social worker and fisherman who regaled anyone who would listen with his wild and hilarious stories. Her maternal grandfather was an artist—a calligrapher, cartoonist, and carpenter—whose gifts were suppressed by the difficulties of the Great Depression. Her paternal grandfather was an attorney and inveterate gambler who, if her father's account can be trusted, once responded to a judge's twenty-dollar fine for contempt of court by slapping a hundred-dollar bill on the bench and declaring, "Now, Your Honor, I've got four more things to say."

Flannery O'Connor once said, "Anybody who has survived childhood has enough information about life to last him the rest of his days." Penelope J. Stokes says she didn't need a full childhood to gather enough ammunition to become a novelist. "All I needed was my DNA!"

Despite her evident destiny, Penny admits it took fifty years, three university degrees, and countless sidetracks to define and refine her sense of gift and calling, to find her own voice in fiction, to learn the craft and skill of writing, to understand herself well enough to understand her characters. "But," she says, "as I sit in my home office day after day, stringing words together on the computer screen, I live with the awareness that this business of being a fiction writer is what I was created to do."

The seed of her calling first sprouted at the age of three or four, when Penny learned to read by looking over her big brother's shoulder as he studied phonetics in first grade. "It was the beginning of a journey into another world, a magical world of words and rhythms, of ideas and wonder," she says. She read everything—the classics, poetry, whatever she could get her hands on. In kindergarten, while the other children were learning their ABC's and being taught how to brush their teeth, Penny was given the job of cataloging the kindergarten library.

She began to seriously consider what it meant to be a writer when she discovered Eudora Welty, who lived in the Belhaven District of Jackson, Mississippi, where Penny grew up. Her father gave her a collection of Welty's short stories when she was eight or nine. "I was fascinated with Welty's characters—the grotesques that populated her work. And I was from the South, so I recognized these folks as authentic." Penny dragged her mother off to Belhaven College for a reading, stood in line to meet Miss Welty, and had her dog-eared copy of Welty's stories autographed. The following year, Penny did a special project on Welty for her English class. "Not knowing any better," she says, "I actually had the audacity to call Eudora Welty up and ask for a telephone interview. She graciously agreed, I got an A on the paper, and I was hooked. It was a watershed event in my young life."

Penelope J. Stokes, writer, was probably born at that moment. But of course, at her young age she had no conviction that this was a calling from God. She believed in God. She was raised Lutheran (which, she says, made her a religious oddball in the Southern Baptist stronghold of the Deep South). She was a religious child, but didn't think of writing as anything religious. "Writing was natural, part of who I was—an outgrowth of my faith, certainly, but part of the seamless fabric of life in the image of God," she says. "It was what I loved—the power and mystery of words, the way they could transport you to another time or place, the way they could create reality out of nothing."

As an adult, Penny now sees the creativity of writing as a kind of parallel to the creativity of God, speaking things into existence by the power of the word. But when she was young, all she knew was that writing was magical, and she gave herself to it heart and soul.

In high school she wrote prodigiously. "I was a literary dweeb," she says, and the dweebiness persisted as she entered college at Mississippi University for Women. "Honoring both my parents," she says, "I took a degree in literature and social work—literature for my soul, social work as a hedge against the inevitable need for gainful employment."

With no job in sight, she went on to grad school, earning first a master's, then a Ph.D. in literature. The immersion in literature fed her spirit and fueled her desire to write. Though she was told she would not be allowed to focus her doctoral program on creative writing, Penny still wanted to be a novelist. "But everywhere I turned, people told me that I'd never make it, that I couldn't generate a living with my creative gift," she says. Her only option seemed to be the one she took: teaching.

She landed a job in a very small Christian college in Memphis. During her first summer in Memphis, a friend convinced her to attend a writers conference. She applied and was accepted, then drove eleven hundred miles by herself to Minnesota for the conference. "I was determined to find out, once and for all, whether I had a chance to make it as a writer," she says. She presented a few of her poems (all she had to offer in the way of creative writing) to a prominent editor at a critique session. He took one look and said, "Go home, kid, you'll never be a writer."

"I was devastated," Penny recalls. She left her meeting with him and went to lunch, still clutching her file folder of poems. Waiting in line, she struck up a conversation with a young man who asked about her writing. She told him a little about herself and showed him a couple of poems, and he asked, "Would you be interested in doing an article?"

Her first response was, "Oh, I don't write articles. I'm a poet."

But the man, who turned out to be senior editor of a large Christian magazine, convinced her she could write articles for him and gave her an assignment. Penelope J. Stokes, professional writer, was on her way just minutes after being told she'd never be a writer!

Other people she met at the conference gave her additional encouragement. Minneapolis, it seemed, had one of the largest and most active Christian writers guilds in the nation. The following year she got a teaching job in Minnesota and moved halfway across the country so she could be in a position to get input on her writing and improve her craft.

For several years she wrote nonfiction articles, taught college writing and literature, and immersed herself in learning what she needed to know about writing for the Christian market. She met people, attended seminars, and developed a network of colleagues all across the country. "Eventually I found myself sitting across a dinner table discussing fiction with one of the best known editors in the business. 'I'd like to do what you do,' I told her. And she gave me a chance."

Penny began to edit novels. After six years as a college professor in Minnesota, she left teaching to work full time on editing. "I loved it, and I discovered I was good at it." It paid the bills, yet the dream still lived. She wanted to write fiction of her own.

Through editing, Penny learned what publishers wanted and what would sell. But after several aborted attempts at writing novels intended to "catch the wave" of current trends in fiction, a close friend of hers did an intervention. She sat Penny down and asked a crucial question: "Where is your passion? If you could write anything, what would it be?"

Immediately Penny knew the answer. It was the story of her parents, a Yankee soldier and a southern belle who met and fell in love during the early years of World War II. She wrote a proposal, hammered out a hundred pages, and received two offers for a three-book contract for her first fiction series. "I learned a very important lesson in the process," she says. "No matter what the trends, I have to write out of my own passion, to tell the story that's burning in my soul."

Looking back, Penny realizes that everything she perceived as hindrances to her dream of being a novelist actually worked to her benefit in the long run. In hindsight she could see that all along,

God had been nudging her, opening doors, confirming the dream in her heart. "All those roadblocks to the dream were actually paths—meandering paths, perhaps, but paths nevertheless—that led me in the direction I was destined to go."

Her education opened doors and gave her a level of respectability, even when she had no background in editing or writing for publication. Her years of studying literature gave her an innate sense of what is good and how writing works. Her college teaching experience prepared her to be an editor, a writer, and a speaker. And all those years of editing everyone else's fiction helped her to learn from other people's mistakes and refine her own writing. "Not to mention," she adds with a chuckle, "establishing me as a kind of 'expert' in Christian fiction."

Her spiritual experiences also shaped Penny as a writer. As a child, she had always loved her Lutheran church—loved the liturgies, the intellectual and spiritual challenges, the questions, the way the rituals and music and mystery pointed her to something beyond herself. She had been raised to believe in God and to think for herself, and she responded with fervor to the Lutheran church's passion for social justice.

But in her second year of college, she met up with some evangelical Christians who told her in no uncertain terms that her Lutheran faith and heritage weren't good enough, that she had to be born again. She didn't have a conversion date she could point to— she had grown up believing in Christ. But she walked down the aisle and committed her life to Jesus. She went home and told her parents she was a Christian now. Their response was predictable: "So what have you been all these years?"

For a number of years after that, Penny's spiritual life was confined to a kind of bumper-sticker theology. "I even had the bumper sticker that said One Way. Unfortunately, what I meant was *our* way of thinking," she admits. "*Our* way of talking. *Our* way of perceiving. We were very, very sure we had all the answers. It was a comforting, if self-deceiving, position."

Several years and "about a million questions later," she says she "emerged back into the blinding light of reality, painfully aware that nobody had all the answers and that I had been pretty arrogant to think that at twenty years of age I had the universe figured out." The lesson has stayed with her, both in her personal life and in her writing. "Today, I try to extend grace and acceptance to those around me and leave the judging to God.

"In my writing, that ongoing search for spiritual truth is, I believe, one of the greatest assets to my calling. I'm constantly reminded by my own religious history that people come to God and understand their relationship with God in a variety of different ways." She believes one of her tasks as a writer is to make her fiction as accessible as possible to the greatest number of people—to present the story, step aside, and allow God to work in her readers' lives to make whatever application or response is needed.

"Writing teachers always tell students 'Write what you know,'" Penny says. "What do I know? I know myself—my struggles, my doubts, my moments of glory and victory, my times of defeat. I know what it means to feel out of place. I know what dreams are made of, and how they can die, or change, or be fulfilled in ways beyond imagining. I know love—not just the heady giddiness of romance, but commitment and friendship and the sometimes difficult interactions with those we call family. I know the love and infinite patience of God, and the thousands of ways God's grace sneaks up on me when I'm not looking. I know that life doesn't always work out the way we want it to. And I know that God brings hope, even during times of darkness and despair."

It is about these things that Penelope Stokes writes. In the end, she says it has been her journey of faith that has informed her fiction and directed her course. "For me, the calling is to live in connection with God and then allow that connection to flow out of me into what I write. I'm reminded often of that famous line from *Chariots of Fire*, when Eric Liddell chooses to go to the Olympics rather than return to the mission field: 'I feel God's pleasure in me when I run.' On my best days, I feel God's pleasure in me when I write."

For you and for me, the calling is the same: to live in connection with God and then allow that connection to flow out of us into our jobs, our relationships, our interactions with others. When we do this, we, too, will feel God's pleasure in us when we do whatever God has gifted us to do.

DEBORAH RANEY

"In my books, I draw heavily from my own experiences as a wife and mother to make the characters of my novels come to life. I set my characters down in the middle of a heart-wrenching dilemma, and then try to imagine how my own faith might carry me through such a trial."

DEBORAH RANEY has published four novels, as well as several nonfiction articles and books, including *More Children's Sermons to Go. A Vow to Cherish* won a 1997 Angel Award for Excellence in Media and was made into a movie that is now available on video and DVD in seven languages. Deborah's short stories have appeared in THE STORYTELLERS' COLLECTION and TEATIME STORIES FOR MOTHERS short story collections. She and her family live in Kansas.

The Gracious Hand of the Lord

Deborah Raney feels she has a dual calling. First and foremost, it's to be a wife and mother. The other more public calling came much later—and was related to her first commitment.

Deborah grew up in the 1970s when women were expected to aspire to be doctors and lawyers. She aspired to be a mother. "I wanted twelve kids," she says. Several doctors told her she probably would not be able to conceive. Within a five-and-a-half-year period, the Lord gave Deborah and her husband two sons and a daughter.

"I was living the life I wanted to live," she says, "but I knew that motherhood was a job with a time limit. When the kids were in college I would need to get a job." When their oldest son, Tarl, was almost fourteen and the other children were ten and eight, she and her husband were surprised by another pregnancy. That little girl was a preschooler when Tarl was ready for college.

Deborah and her husband needed money for college tuition, but she also wanted to be home for her young daughter. What to do? She thought back on what she had loved to do when she was younger. She had always gravitated toward writing, though she had not studied it formally beyond three semesters of college. What else did she know? She had worked as an occupational therapist's assistant for a couple of years after college and getting married. Could there be something in that?

One day she had a conversation with her husband and older children about Alzheimer's disease. It seemed that everywhere she turned, she was hearing about that issue. A family friend and several grandparents of her children's friends were struggling with the disease. Former president Ronald Reagan's Alzheimer's diagnosis had recently brought the disease to wide national attention.

Deborah was fascinated by the different perspectives her children brought to the conversation. That night, as she lay in bed thinking about the things they'd discussed, a story began to take shape in her mind.

It was December 1993. At the bottom of her list of New Year's resolutions for 1994, she added, "Write the book." On January 1, she wrote the prologue. Her husband read it and told her he was very impressed. A few days later, he bought Deborah a computer to use for her writing.

"That first story, *A Vow to Cherish*, poured out of me," Deborah says. By May the story was ready for a publisher. She sent it out but received some rejections. "My husband had written children's books, and he had received more than eighty rejections," Deborah says. "So I knew they were to be expected."

She got a call from a small publisher in New York one day. The contact person said they loved the book, but offered a very small amount of money. In the following few weeks, two different Christian publishers called. When Bethany House Publishers offered her a two-book contract, she knew they were the right choice. "The amount they offered was to the penny what we had just been told our son's college tuition, room, and board would be. To me it was confirmation that I was going in the right direction." After all, hadn't she turned to writing mainly to pay for college tuition?

God had other plans for Deborah and for that book. Billy Graham's film company, World Wide Pictures, made a movie based on the story. It aired on television on Labor Day weekend in 1999. It's also on video and DVD in six languages besides English. Deborah was told after the movie aired that the Billy Graham organization was receiving five hundred email messages a day from people whose lives had been touched by the film. That strikes awe into Deborah. "I had so little to do with that film," she says, "so I feel I can brag on it. I was only a tiny seed for that project; they made a lot of changes and added a strong salvation message to the plot. It's amazing to think that God could take this uneducated Kansas housewife and do something like that through me." All in response to her need for college tuition and Deborah's faithfulness to her first calling as a mother.

A Vow to Cherish launched Deborah's writing career, which also led to something she'd always dreamed of: public speaking. "Speaking was something I had always wanted to do but never felt I had the experience," she says. "Because of my writing, people began to approach me about speaking. Writing not only paid for my kids' college education, but it opened another new door for me."

Though she enjoys the speaking, Deborah is very clear that for now, writing takes priority. She writes when her daughter is in school, usually working for three weeks straight and then taking one or two weeks off to catch up on friendships and household projects. She also tries to take the summers off. "Too much coming and going in our house to get much writing done then," she says. She's still a mother first, a writer second.

Deborah now sees how God's hand of grace was on her even when she didn't know what he wanted her to do. For instance, when she worked with Alzheimer's patients as an occupational therapist's assistant for those two years, she had no idea she was doing research for a future book. Even the writing process—what to include or leave out—was apparently guided by God's hand, as she found out from a letter from a prisoner.

Bethany House Publishers sends many of their damaged or remaindered books to prisons. One day, a prisoner in solitary confinement, who was serving time for murder, decided to try one of the "God books" he'd always refused when the book cart came by. It was a novel by Robert Funderburk. He read it and was surprised that he liked it. The next day he read a Gilbert Morris book. On the third day, he picked up *A Vow to Cherish*. Toward the end of a book, a character named John is sitting at his son's wedding. He had been tempted to start a relationship with another woman after his wife developed Alzheimer's disease. As his son and his son's fiancée said their vows, he realized he had made those same vows to his wife. As he resolved to do the right thing, the sun came through the clouds and shone through the stained glass windows of the church.

The prisoner wrote to Deborah that when he read that part of the book, the Lord reminded him of a vow he had made to God early in his life. And as he thought about that, the sun, which had been obscured by rain clouds all day, broke through the window of the prison cell and shone right on a Bible. The prisoner started reading that Bible that day, and he wrote a four-page letter to Bethany House to tell all about how the Lord was dealing with him.

"I almost didn't include that part about the sun shining in that scene in the book," Deborah says. "When I read that prisoner's letter, I sat at my desk and just sobbed. I told the Lord, 'If nothing else ever comes from that book, it was worth it just for that one prisoner.'"

It's all intertwined, Deborah says. "The Lord uses a ministry like Bethany House to not only reach out to prisoners, but to provide a way for me to put shoes on my kids' feet and pay for their college tuition. He gave me the desire to be a wife and mother, then used that to lead me to certain stories to write about. I love writing, and people are blessed by the stories I write. What a wonderful circle of blessings. God is so good!"

When the gracious hand of the Lord is upon a person, blessings abound, blessings that reach to eternity.